"*Get Them on Your Side* by Samuel B. Bacharach makes a brilliant case for building political competence in leaders. Read, practice, and enjoy undreamed-of results."

—Ken Blanchard, coauthor of
The One-Minute Manager and *The Secret*

"Having been involved in fourteen startups, including FedEx, it is clear to me that innovation is a combination of concept and commitment. Of the two, commitment is, far and away, the most important ingredient. Bacharach shows you how to gain the commitment necessary for success. He debunks the myth that all company politics are bad. In fact, without what he calls 'political competence,' very little innovation would ever happen. Read this book if you want your ideas to become corporate breakthroughs."

—Michael Basch, FedEx founding Sr. Vice President;
author of *CustomerCulture*

"The principles and processes presented in this book go far beyond the workplace. While much of the book is directed to the workplace, the principles can be applied to almost any relationship. I found this book extremely useful and one of the best three-hour reads I've had in a very long time."

—Alan Swerdloff, Vice President,
Bernstein Investment Research and Management

"This smart, readable book makes an often slippery topic understandable. Through stories we all recognize, and crisp management suggestions, Professor Bacharach offers some simple ways to effectively get support for making things happen. For anyone who has ever seen a great idea slip away into the organizational void, the lessons offered here will help you actually get those ideas implemented. In the 'execution era,' these are invaluable skills."

—Martha E. Sherman, Vice President,
Human Resources, JPMorgan Chase & Co.

Praise for *Get Them on Your Side*

"I found *Get Them on Your Side* surprisingly reflective of the things I do as a fire officer on the frontline and as a president of a union. I live in a world of crisis, and Bacharach shows how leaders can work with people to bring order to chaos.

"Unions are traditionally opposed to new ideas. The successful union leader needs not only new ideas but the tools necessary to win support of both labor and management. This book provides the step-by-step analysis of how to work with people with different mindsets in order to achieve success.

"Finally, someone has written a logical step-by-step book that navigates the reader through the process of attaining success. I found this book to be extremely insightful and useful."

—Peter Gorman, President,
Uniformed Fire Officers Association, New York City

"Samuel Bacharach understands the essential ingredients that organizational change requires. *Get Them on Your Side* effectively outlines the frameworks, spectrum of approaches, coalition requirements, and personal credibility that managers at all levels must master as leaders of change. Most importantly, Samuel Bacharach describes the essence of successful change—the mastery of political competence. In a world that knows the aberrations that mismanaged change creates, everyone should take note of this important guide to successful change management."

—John Hofmeister, HR Director, Royal Dutch Shell

"Professor Bacharach has tackled a difficult and important topic that those of us who work in executive circles encounter almost daily. His work sheds new light on the importance of understanding, mapping, and dealing with the political realities in any organizational system. Moreover, he helps us understand what political competence entails, as well as how it can be developed and used to great advantage in getting ideas accepted and changes made within almost any organizational setting."

—Jon R. Katzenbach, Director, Katzenbach Partners, LLC,
author of *Teams at the Top* and *Why Pride Matters More Than Money*

Praise for *Get Them on Your Side*

"This book starts where Fisher and Ury's *Getting to Yes* and Bossidy and Charan's *Execution* left off. In contrast to all previous books, Bacharach shows how execution in organizations requires knowledge of how to manage conflict and move people along. In this extremely readable volume, Bacharach redefines the very notion of organizational politics, making political skill a usable and practical tool. This book should be required reading for anyone interested in negotiation, mediation, conflict resolution, and the pragmatics of organizational life."

—David B. Lipsky, President-Elect,
Labor and Employment Relations Association
(formerly the Industrial Relations Research Association);
coauthor of *Emerging Systems for Managing Workplace Conflict*

"Had I read this book twenty years ago, it would have saved me a lot of headaches and a lot of trouble. This book does a great job in laying out the specific steps that one has to follow in order to succeed in organizations. Bacharach's idea of political competence and his understanding of how to create and use coalitions is the key to getting things done in all organizations. I apply these concepts in my daily work dealing with clients, colleagues, government agencies, and foundations. This engaging volume brings political competence to the forefront. This book gives us real skills for the real world."

—Shirley Traylor, Executive Director, Harlem Legal Services, Inc.

"Sam Bacharach is one of those unique academics who has the ability to take complex ideas and make them work in the day-to-day world of practice. This book is testimony to that skill. While academically based, it is written with humor and good sense. Bacharach understands the politics of organizations and the specific skills required to make things happen. I would prescribe this book as a guide to anyone concerned with getting something done in any organization. Not since Fisher and Ury's *Getting to Yes* have I read a volume that is more practical and immediate in its implications. This is a gem that should be read by most everyone. It will change what you think it means to be political."

—Edward J. Lawler, Martin P. Catherwood Professor;
Dean, School of Industrial and Labor Relations

Praise for *Get Them on Your Side*

"Bacharach's new book couldn't be more timely or more on target. He provides sophisticated and essential advice in straightforward terms to help us all overcome organizational barriers and get things done successfully at work, at school, in the neighborhood, or anywhere else social organizations operate. Rather than bemoan the politics of organizations, he enriches us with the knowledge to navigate those politics by leveraging the power of coalition-building with the people around us. This book is a must-read for anyone seeking a whole new perspective on managing life in uncertain times and complex organizations."

—Stephen Keyes, Esq., Vice President,
Compensation, Limited Brands, Inc.

"This book is a must-read. When it comes to the politics of coalitions and how to get things done, Sam Bacharach is the leading academic expert. This book is readable, engaging, and very important. He takes his years of expertise and puts it into a language that we can all understand. He takes his theories and ideas that have grown out of his academic work and applies them to a real-world setting. This book is of immense importance to anyone who understands that nothing gets done unless you make it happen. This book is critical to those individuals— managers, union leaders, community leaders, politicians—who understand that leadership is about having the appropriate political skills. For the first time, we have a book that shows us that leadership involves specific political skills that we can all learn. The message of this book is for not only those with power, but those who aspire to get ahead. I would recommend this book particularly to women and minorities who are concerned with pushing important agendas."

—Ida Torres, President,
Hispanic Labor Committee, New York City AFL-CIO

"'Political competence' as discussed in this book is what I do every day as the head of an advocacy organization. This is the first book ever to specify what the necessary skills are to achieve political competence. In order to succeed, in order to get them on your side, in order to create change, you need to develop a set of political leadership skills. While everyone may know this, this book does a superb job at specifying what skills you need, what processes you need to engage in order to succeed. If you understand that a good idea is simply not enough to assure success, if you understand that you live in a political world, you must read this book."

—Stacia Murphy, President,
National Council on Alcoholism and Drug Dependence

Praise for *Get Them on Your Side*

"This book brings out the forgotten skill of political competence and puts it on the table in front of all of us. Bacharach understands that leading has a lot to do with one's political skills. Unlike any volume I've ever read, he shows us that the political skills leaders—managers, human resource directors, principals of schools, community leaders, CEOs, salespeople—need are skills that can be learned. He understands the reality of organizations and the practical skills one needs to succeed. This book is a resource I am recommending to my clients to assist them with their development and growth in their positions. This is a very important and readable book."

—Anthony Panos, President, Performance Training (Shelton, CT)

"This book made me aware of the dynamics and politics involved in getting things done and being a proactive leader. Bacharach, who has a thirty-year reputation as a researcher, takes his academic knowledge and makes it relevant to real-world practitioners. In this accessible book, he has convinced me that everyone can learn the political skills necessary to get things done. This book is both sophisticated and straightforward. It should be welcome on any practitioner's desk."

—Deniz Omurgonulsen, Training Manager,
The Pierre, a Four Seasons Hotel, New York, NY

"*Get Them on Your Side* is a thoughtful and well-organized manual for those who seek to have their ideas heard and implemented. Author Samuel B. Bacharach draws on the literature of negotiation theory, political theory, and organization development, as well as his own research and experience, to create a highly readable, step-by-step guide to effective leadership within organizations and communities."

—Nancy E. Peace, Past President, Association for Conflict Resolution; Instructor,
Negotiating Labor Agreements: New Strategies for Achieving Better Collective
Bargaining Outcomes, Program on Negotiation at Harvard Law School and Institute for
Work and Employment Research, Massachusetts Institute of Technology

"*Get Them on Your Side* teaches us why we all need to develop political skills. It's an especially useful book if you feel that it's time your ideas were accepted, not just heard, that it's time to lead, not just participate. So, if you need to overcome roadblocks and obstacles to your ideas and agenda—read this book!"

—M. Cindy Hounsell, Executive Director,
Women's Institute for a Secure Retirement

Praise for *Get Them on Your Side*

"Enlisting people to help you overcome obstacles is the challenge of a leader. In over thirty years with the Chicago Police Department, I've learned that when you need to put people in harm's way, you have to make sure that they believe in you and your ideas. You need to be on their side and they need to be on yours. In this insightful and useful book, Samuel Bacharach specifies what you need to do in order to build coalitions that produce results and make you a successful leader. I would recommend this book to anyone who needs to build support and take action."

—John W. Richardson, Jr., Former Deputy Superintendent,
Chicago Police Department

"The outstanding idea often fades away unless the sponsor can successfully gain support throughout the organization to make the idea a reality. Sam Bacharach outlines several requirements to rally the organization behind the idea and to translate the initiative into action and explains the realities of gaining support for new initiatives in the organization and the action steps required to insure the initiative is implemented successfully. Bacharach illustrates how his requirements contribute to success or failure if not followed. The book will be useful to all managers who are responsible for new initiatives, particularly managers who have joined new organizations."

—Douglas M. Reid, Senior Vice President,
Human Resources, PanAmSat Corporation

"The book presents an extremely useful blueprint on how to affect change in an organization—without any silly references to mice and cheese. I wish I had read *Get Them on Your Side* prior to banging my head against the wall for six years in the corporate world! I also believe that [Bacharach's] strategy will be useful to me in my daily practice of law, as a significant part of what I do is trying to get organizational clients to accept my advice."

—Anthony J. Amendola, Senior Partner,
Mitchell Silberberg & Knupp LLP

GET
THEM
ON YOUR
SIDE

SAMUEL B. BACHARACH

Director of Cornell University's Institute for Workplace Studies

PLATINUM
PRESS™

Avon, Massachusetts

For Yael and Ben
Thank you for being on my side
. . .

Published by Platinum Press™, an imprint of
Adams Media, an F+W Publications Company
57 Littlefield Street, Avon, MA 02322. U.S.A.
www.adamsmedia.com

Platinum Press™ is a trademark of F+W Publications, Inc.

ISBN 10: 1-59337-736-3
ISBN 13: 978-1-59337-736-6
Printed in the United States of America.

Library of Congress Cataloging-in-Publication Data
Bacharach, Samuel B.
Get them on your side / Samuel B. Bacharach.
p.   cm.
ISBN 1-59337-736-3 (paperback)
ISBN 1-59337-278-7 (hardcover)
1. Organizational behavior. I. Title.
HD58.7.B3415 2005
658.4'095—dc22
2004026357

Cover illustration by Mada Design.
Interior illustrations by Argosy.

This book is available at quantity discounts for bulk purchases.
For information, please call 1-800-289-0963.

Contents

Acknowledgments

This book represents the collective input of several hundred people. On the top of the list are my various students. I am especially grateful to the students who, over the last ten years, have participated in seminars and workshops that have helped me define the ideas contained in this volume. These students came from a rich background. Some were corporate executives, social workers, teachers, principals, psychologists, human resource specialists, secret service agents, diplomats, high-tech entrepreneurs, academics, engineers, school administrators, community organizers, politicians, undergraduates, and graduates. Some had many years of experience; some had very few years of experience. They came from many countries, with a variety of experience. All of them understood, and helped me to understand, that in order to get things done, you have to be proactive. In order to move an idea, you have to get people on your side. The dialogue with these students has taught me well.

Throughout my years at Cornell, I have been helped by a number of special people, including Sue Besemer, Colleen Clauson, Marsha Cox, Jackie Dodge, Gail Hendrix, Anita Henry-Wilkins, Sandy Jordan, Krista Knout, Pam Kline, Barb McPherson, Pat Welch, and Theresa Woodhouse.

I have deep gratitude for the Smithers Foundation, especially Adele and Christopher, who for the last decade have given me the opportunity to do the type of work that I truly find meaningful.

Esta Bigler and Charlie McCorkle have been of great support throughout this process. My gratitude to Siegfried Altscher, whose real-world experience was invaluable at a critical point in this project. Catherine Silver and Seymour Spilerman have always encouraged me to feel comfortable outside the academic box. Yael Stark Bacharach read numerous drafts of this volume and provided a real-world perspective.

Tony and Paula Panos gave me excellent assistance as I tried to work my way through the book. Francis N. Bonsignore, Richard Singer, and Steve Keyes were early readers of the volume. Their insight was critical to the book's development. Francis's role as one of the most senior human resource executives in the country and Richard's role as a union leader gave me balance and tremendous insight. Steve Keyes's sense of the pragmatic and what is useful kept me focused. Stuart Basefsky, being the superb master of information he is, was an ally throughout this process.

Sara Edwards has the capacity of asking the uncomfortable questions which pushed me further. Fil Sanna was an important source of focus early in this project. David Yantonro was not only a good source of ideas but brought his entire graphic design touch to the material and the underlying logic of the book. Hilary Zelko was extremely patient, as she understood that this book would never succeed if I kept lecturing like an academic. Val McKinney has always been a superb colleague, a brilliant reader, and a good friend. Kirsten Amann was really indispensable in bringing this project to its completion. I would like to thank Jill Alexander for her thoughtful attention to this project. She's been a real advocate. Edward Knappman made this project possible. He is extremely insightful, supportive, and a superb master of the English language. John Neuman quickly understood the applicability of this project and really helped to make it happen.

David Lipsky for years has believed in my ideas, sometimes more than I did, giving me the confidence to move ahead. David is the type of friend that always goes the extra mile.

Amos Drory gave me an opportunity to engage in creative executive teaching, which incubated the ideas contained in this volume. Gil Luria, who for the last six years has assisted me in my desert seminars, has been more than an ally. His unique focus, discipline, and persistence kept us both going. Peter Bamberger has been a research collaborator and coauthor for over two decades, creating opportunity and pushing me to get things done I didn't think I was capable of doing.

William Sonnenstuhl, professor of organizational behavior at Cornell, has been a dear friend, a superb colleague, and a first-rate critic of my efforts. Bill is an academic colleague who understands friendship and community. Had Bill not encouraged me to write this book, I'm not sure I would have.

Edward Lawler deserves a very special thanks. He's been my friend and colleague for thirty-five years, always supplying brilliant insight, great advice, and constant support. It is a long way since his wife, Joan, Ed, and I met in Madison, Wisconsin—a road well traveled together.

Then when it came to the crunch there was Jim Biolos and Katie Briggs, the type of people who know your limitations and help you overcome them. Jim generously shared his imagination and work experience to help bring these ideas to light. Jim's insight constantly amazed me. His role in helping to develop the arguments and the cases has been invaluable. He has a unique capacity for taking abstract ideas and grounding them in the real world. Without Katie Briggs's analytical skills, focus, and friendship, this project could not have been completed. Not only is she a superb coordinator and strategist, she is simply one of the most gifted writers and diligent editors I've ever known. I'm delighted to have these people on my side.

Then there are those who really understood the world. They are not academics, not theoreticians, but pragmatists and realists in the best sense of the word: Martin and Shari Stark, who exemplify the talent of building again; Lina Wind, who was a model of continuity; and my parents, Hanna and Martin Bacharach, who as working immigrants understood that survival and success depend not simply on having good ideas, but the skills to get people on your side. Theirs is a generation of survivors.

Introduction

A Good Idea Is Not Enough:
You Need Political Competence

D id you ever have the feeling that you knew exactly what had to be done in your organization (be it at your office, school, union, political party, neighborhood—wherever your job or life interests take you), but you just couldn't get others to go along with you? Did you ever have the feeling that others—whose ideas maybe aren't as good as yours—are capable of getting their agendas adopted, while you constantly run into roadblocks whenever you try to get a group of people to agree with you? Why is it that even though you usually have great ideas, others seem to be able to get people to join their bandwagon, while you end up standing on the sidelines watching the parade pass by? Have you tried to follow what the experts say about how to execute, implement, and manage change and still come up short? How is it that others can get people on their side and win support, convert skeptics, and get results?

Some would claim that good leadership is dependent on good ideas. The notion that a good idea will carry the day is the touchstone of all action in organizations. It's a comforting myth. We'd all like to believe that if we come up with a great idea everyone will rally around our insight and wisdom and that reason will prevail. As anyone working in an organization knows, good ideas are usually not enough to win the day.

People who push ideas that never get off the ground may become organizational casualties. Their idea may get crushed by opposition before it has a chance to be implemented. On the other hand, successful leaders not only push an idea, but they also understand the opposition, get people on their side, and get results. Maybe—just maybe—the difference between casualties and successful leaders is not a question of which one has a better idea, but a question of their *political competence*.

There is no shortage of good ideas. The problem is how to turn good ideas into action. It is easy for someone to tell you that you need to change how you deal with your customer, how you measure your outputs, how you approach organizational culture, how you recruit and compensate employees, and how you focus on your core technology. But it is difficult to know how to put these ideas in place—how to get results. Many people know what needs to be done, but few are able to leverage the energy and support of others in order to do it.

Power may be seen as getting people to do something in spite of their resistance. Some would maintain that if you have the authority, the knowledge, or the resources to make you powerful, you'll be able to push your agenda through the organization.* But think about it—how often have you seen people who were powerful and yet still failed? The question is not only one of power, but also one of political competence. Power without political competence may achieve some short-term success, but it is likely to doom you to long-term failure. On the other hand, political competence may allow for the success of those who are not obviously powerful in the organization. The premise of this book is that the key to empowering individuals to get results in an organization is not simply a matter of giving them more power, more input, or decision-making authority. The key to true empowerment is the development of political competence.

What differentiates someone who can get results in their job, school, neighborhood, church—wherever—from someone who can't? Both may have equal power, the same idea, the same strategic plan, the same background knowledge, the same interest in teamwork, but the one who makes things happen is the one who is situationally aware—the one who knows,

---

* Weber's definition of power ["Power is the probability that one actor within a social relationship will be in a position to carry out his own will, despite resistance, and regardless of the basis on which this probability rests." Max Weber, *The Theory of Social and Economic Organization*, (Oxford University Press, 1947)] implies the notion that to be powerful, one has to have a way of overcoming resistance. In the context of our discussion here, one needs a way of moving people to one's side. See also French and Raven, "The bases of social power," in D. Cartwright and A. Zander (eds.), *Group Dynamics* (Harper & Row, 1960).

anticipates, and reacts to the interests, agendas, and intentions of others in the organization. A quarterback may have a great arm, but if he fails to be aware of the entire field then he won't succeed. Those who make things happen in organizations must have a similar broader field of vision.

Making things happen depends on your broad political vision. It isn't simply a matter of getting a good idea, laying out a plan, telling others what to do, and overseeing the implementation. In order to get results you have to *identify allies and resistors*, you have to *get the buy-in*, you have to *build coalitions*, and you have to *lead politically*.

A good idea, a great idea, a mediocre idea—no matter what kind of idea you have, before you lay off those six people in Detroit, or rearrange the furniture in the upstairs conference room, or install a new server, you have to do your political homework. *You need political competence.*

Political competence is the ability to understand what you can and cannot control, when to take action, anticipate who is going to resist your agenda, and determine whom you need on your side to push your agenda forward. Political competence is about knowing how to map the political terrain, get others on your side, and lead coalitions. More often than not, political competence is not understood as a critical core competence that is needed by all leaders in organizations.

When you ask successful leaders how they get results, they'll talk to you about brainstorming, participation, leadership, market analysis, and planning, but they'll rarely elaborate on the perpetual day-to-day micro-politics they engage in. If they dared to speak it, the truth might go something like this:

> *First I got together with Joe, who I knew was going to be one of the bigger pains in the neck around here because he's been here forever. We didn't talk about specifics. He likes talking about generalities. Then I talked to Mary who tends to be more of a nuts-and-bolts person. And when I was able to get a buy-in from both of them, I was able to leverage that to get some more political backing. Look, I knew the notion of consolidating the HR function was going to cross turf. There was no way I was going to take a chance of being left out to dry if it didn't work. Hell, I'm not even sure in this market if we can afford an HR office. All in all, this was all a question of politics.*

People in organizations today worry about their personal vulnerability. You operate in an environment where those in authority maintain that they want your input and cling to the political correctness of involvement and participation, while you worry about what will happen, if, by chance, your suggestions are wrong. You live in a world where you want to stand out as an individual, but not too much. In organizational life you want to be given credit in the case of success, but you also want to share responsibility and accountability if things don't quite go right. We all know that organizations are political arenas of individual, subgroup, and organizational interests. Such organizations are arenas in which interests are often not in harmony, and they frequently collide. However, despite its importance, politics seems to be a taboo subject in organizational life—the elephant in the living room that no one discusses or admits is there.*

Political competence is not an evil by-product of organizational life. Being political, in its most attractive light, is being aware of the interests of others, finding areas of common ground, bringing others on board, and leading them in the pursuit of a goal. Politics is part and parcel of making things happen in organizations. You need political competence if you are:

- A corporate executive deciding which division to cut
- A principal implementing a new reading program for the third grade
- An assistant professor struggling for tenure
- A human resources manager pushing for a change in the recruiting policy
- A marketing director going after a new niche
- A general attempting to change military communications
- A young officer questioning orders
- A politician trying to get support for your proposed budget

---

* Regarding the elephant in the living room, there has in fact been some academic work on politics in organizations, including Jeffrey Pfeffer's *Managing with Power: Politics and Influence in Organizations* (Harvard Business School Press, 1992), John Kotter's *Power and Influence: Beyond Formal Authority* (Free Press, 1985) and S. B. Bacharach and E. J. Lawler, *Power and Politics in Organizations* (Jossey-Bass, 1980).

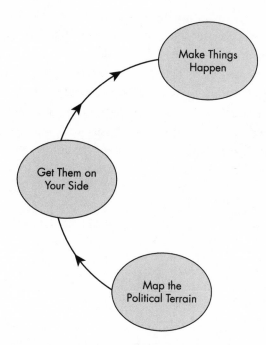

In all of these situations, you need political competence to survive. Without political competence, you can have the best of intentions, the most brilliant of ideas, and the most exquisite processes of execution, but you'll be unlikely to succeed in making things happen in your organization. Political competence is not simply one more process; it is your capacity to understand and analyze your environment—and to take action.

In the organizational world of imperfect decisions, it is political competence that makes things happen. It is your political competence that will translate ideas into action and strategy into results. This volume will teach you how to *map your political terrain, get others on your side, and make things happen*. This volume will introduce you to the practical skills you need to develop and the processes you need to follow in order to achieve political competence and get results.

Part I

Map the
Political Terrain

Chapter 1

Anticipate Reaction

Any idea you have for an organization is based on your own unique interpretation of the organization's past, present, and future. Other individuals and groups will perceive and frame the organization's circumstances differently, based on their past experiences and perceptions of the future. There is no such thing as a common prism. Everyone is coming from a different place.

Sometimes when you make a suggestion or try to push an idea, you'll be met with a deafening silence. You'll wonder if anyone even heard you. You'll be perplexed—"Did they get my e-mail?" . . . "It's been three weeks since I met with the trustees. And still, no reaction." You'll stand at the well, drop in your pebble, wait to hear the distant splash, and hear nothing. It is as if you never tossed the pebble in the first place. Silence itself can be a deathblow. After a while, you'll begin to wonder if you ever met with the board. "If they want me to forget this idea, why don't they tell me?" No matter how deep the silence, you'll have to follow up and force a reaction.

More often than not, any proposal you make will be met not by deafening silence, but by alternative analyses regarding the organization's problems, the causes of those problems, and the appropriate resolutions to those problems. You are vulnerable to criticism whenever you propose an idea. For every decision you make, for every initiative you launch, there will be pockets of resistance and criticism directed toward your idea and toward you personally. Political competence requires that you anticipate what they are going to say.*

Take the case of Sobel Wines. In 1932, at the age of sixteen, Manny (Emmanuel) Sobel began his kosher wine vineyard in upstate New York. From the 1930s through the 1960s, Sobel's winery did very well in its market. In September 1971, just before the Jewish New Year, Manny was rushed to the hospital with liver failure. Because his sons were too young to take over the firm, Manny hired Art Goldberg, the son of his childhood friend, as the new CEO of Sobel Wines.

---

* The basic ideas in this chapter owe a lot to the work of Albert O. Hirschman in *The Rhetoric of Reaction: Perversity, Futility, Jeopardy* (Harvard University Press, 1991). Hirschman identifies three generic arguments that skeptics use to oppose change: perversity, futility, and jeopardy. Analyzing the reaction to the liberal ideas of the French Revolution and the Declaration of the Rights of Man, Hirschman illustrates these three arguments by examining the works of different writers of the time. Hirschman examines ideas in their historical context, which can be reformulated in an organizational context.

Under Art's diligent direction during the 1980s and 1990s, the winery built distribution nationally and grew substantially. In 1998, Art, ailing from coronary disease, underwent a quadruple bypass. At sixty-nine, he knew he should retire. He needed to name a successor.

Naturally, Art considered members of the Sobel family for the top spot. David, Manny's eldest son who ran the company's store on the Lower East Side, remained uninterested in leading the company. Manny's daughter, Sara, forty-eight years old and a mother of three, was too busy with her own life to run the company. Marc (forty-four) wanted to be the CEO. Art, however, thought that Marc didn't have a well-rounded understanding of the business and wasn't quite ready to lead the organization.

Art put his feelers outside the organization and brought in Troy Wadsworth (fifty-three), a seasoned wine executive. Troy, a graduate of Boston College and with a master's from the School of Hotel Administration at Cornell University, had worked for a respected California winery for twenty years, where he worked his way up to product management of the winery's successful entry into high-end wines. In 1988, he assumed the position of executive vice president of Montevideo wines. His charter was to expand the Montevideo business internationally. Art believed Troy was the guy who would teach the family how to run a successful wine business—so that each could pursue his or her individual interests, while the value of the shares in the company grew. In the end, the siblings reluctantly supported Art's decision to hire Troy.

After barely three months, Troy had run into nothing but problems and roadblocks. Some he could have predicted before he accepted the job, but others threw him for a loop. Sobel's business slowed, and the prospects for the future were bleak. Troy was under a lot of pressure and faced increasing criticism. His prior success, knowledge, and experience bought him a temporary reprieve with the family and the firm's managers, but his goodwill was running out.

After a thorough analysis of the business, Troy dropped the bombshell at a senior management meeting: Sobel Wines needed to move out of the pedestrian Concord grape wine business and into high-end kosher Chardonnays and other fine varietals.

Common objection #1:
"Your idea is too risky."

As soon as you propose a new idea some of your colleagues are likely to try to throw you off course by suggesting that it will put the organization in danger, threatening its highly valued accomplishments and successes. They prefer to play it safe. They just don't want to take a chance, or they just don't want to spend the money.

You know the type. They look you in the face. They cup their hands under their chin sincerely, purse their lips thoughtfully, and quietly shake their head up and down to reassure you. They catch you a bit off guard as they tell you emphatically, "You know, it seems a bit risky." The phrase comes out of their mouth as if it emanates from their innermost self. With these few words, they fertilize any seed of doubt you may have about your idea. To them, the uncertainty involved is so overwhelming that embarking on a new idea is not worth the risk.

❧

At forty-eight, Sara wasn't looking to break new ground. Her father's drinking problem and her radical years at Wellesley made her openly critical of being part of the male-dominated wine business. She continued to work as the marketing head, but she had no further ambition. She talked about leaving the business altogether, as it compromised her values.

When Troy presented his idea, Sara went ballistic. "Troy, do you have any idea how risky that is? We don't know a thing about high-end wines. It would require opening up an entire new distribution system. We'd have to engage with new suppliers and start from scratch with a totally new and expanded marketing effort. Do you realize how expensive that will be? And what if it fails?"

"Sara, I understand your concerns. But you have to understand that our Concord grape business is shrinking."

"I get the idea, but there's a difference between making modifications and corrections to our existing business and getting into an entirely new business. We're not in a position to place a bet like that."

Common objection #2:
"That idea will actually make things worse."

You definitely thought that your idea would work. But after hearing the risk argument, you have a sinking sense that you haven't thought your idea through. Your good idea could be, in fact, a danger to everyone. When the naysayers are most effective, you almost want to thank them for saving the organization and your career from disaster, but all they've done is stop you cold in your tracks.

A common technique used to stop a new idea before it has a chance is to argue that the move will not produce the intended result, but rather, the exact opposite. "This idea is just going to backfire—it will make things worse instead of better."

In this instance, they don't shake their head up and down. They don't even move it from side to side. They simply stare you in the face, with steel-eyed certainty, and tell you that your idea is going to make things worse. They counter your proposal with a sense of their own assurance, their own knowledge, and their own certainty. They try to enlighten you to perspectives, angles, and horizons you didn't anticipate. Their favorite metaphor is that of the boomerang—how your idea will come back and knock your teeth out.

They see your idea as triggering a series of interactive events that will inevitably lead to a world-class catastrophe. Or they will use the domino analogy—if you move one piece the whole project will be destroyed.

≈

David Sobel reacted to Troy's proposal as violently as Sara did. "You gotta be kidding! If we did that, do you know what would happen to our Concord grape business? We'd lose half our retailers. They'd think we're going upmarket and will probably think they are overpaying for the good ol' grape wine. I remember talking about this at a recent wine retailer's association meeting. You can't imagine the disdain that retailers have for the upscale kosher wine distributors. They'll revolt, Troy. I'm telling you, you need to think twice about this idea of yours.

"Not only are we going to spend a ton of money to get it off the ground, we're going to take a hit on sales with our core product. I'm afraid your proposal is actually going to do more damage than good."

Common objection #3:
"Your proposal won't change a thing."

Any time you have a new idea or want to take some action, someone can always come up with a doomsday scenario. In the most dramatic situation, your idea could put the company out of business; in the most benign one, it will merely reduce sales, market share, competitive advantage, or profitability. Your challenge is to recognize this, prepare for it, and respond.

One popular way to stamp out a new idea is to call the effort a waste of time. The suggestion is that any attempt at change will be illusory, a façade, or simply cosmetic.

Your critics will sigh heavily and be reflective as they tell you that based on the organizational history, nothing is going to change. No matter how experienced you are, they will make you feel less experienced. They will cup their hands behind their head, lean back in their chair, and look to the ceiling as if they've been through all of this before. They'll instill in you a sense of futility, that it's all been tried before and that there is no reason to act in haste. There is a sense of inevitability that nothing can be changed, so nobody should waste effort trying.

ॐ

Marc, Manny's youngest son with aspirations to take over the company, was the last Sobel sibling to chime in. "Troy, why do you think that a high-end wine business is the answer to our problems? That'll be like dipping your hand in one cookie jar, only to put the cookie in another jar. You really don't expect your plan to radically change the growth prospects of this business, do you? The only thing that will do is get us invited to next year's *Gourmet* magazine holiday party. I think we need to put our heads together to come up with a plan that can really have a major impact on our long-term growth."

Common objection #4:
"You don't know the issues well enough."

Some may dispute how the issue is cast or the goals of the initiative. You may hear: "You're missing the whole point; the real issue is . . ." Or, your critics may challenge your decision and maintain that a nondecision would have been more appropriate. For example: "You should've waited on that decision to move the computer center to the third floor." Or, "You don't know enough about Chicago to restructure our marketing efforts there."

Organizations today are porous. They have multiple centers and ideas can emerge at many different intersections—not simply in functionally defined units with specific boundaries. Ideas can emerge from anywhere. (This concept is developed in the book by Ron Ashkenas et al. titled *The Boundaryless Organization: Breaking the Chains of Organizational Structure* [Jossey-Bass, 1998].) At one time, the leader of any initiative was typically the person who had the most expertise in the organization about that particular topic. Not anymore. More often, people taking action and leading efforts do not have the deep technical knowledge or years of experience in the particular field where they are driving change. Frequently, those who do have the technical knowledge or expertise report to them or are in another part of the organization.

Because of this, you will inevitably face the criticism that "you don't know . . ." or that "you're not a marketing director, so you cannot lead this effort." Consider the situation at a large metropolitan hospital, where a young nurse practitioner is trying to push for changes in the way medication is dispensed to nurses and attendants in the intensive care unit. As this nurse practitioner begins to make her agenda more apparent, she will likely face criticism that sounds like: "She's only been in this hospital for nine months—she just doesn't understand how we operate." Or, "She's not an RN or a doctor—what does she know about dispensing medicine?"

These are not criticisms of your idea (although stopping your idea is likely to be the main goal of your detractors), but denunciations of you as the leader of the initiative. The strategy employed by these detractors is to attempt to derail your effort by reducing your credibility or legitimacy as the leader of this effort.

❧

Dakota Sobel, David's eldest son, was the company's sales manager. Dakota was deeply troubled by Troy's proposal. "Troy, you have a lot more experience than I do with selling mass-market wines. But this is the kosher wine business. It's different. Buyers have very different criteria and make their purchase decision very differently than they do with front-of-the-store wines. Listen, I've been selling our stuff for six years now—I know our customers and you don't. They won't go for it, Troy. If you spoke to them and dealt with them every day, the way I do, you'd understand the problem with your idea."

Common objection #5:
"You're doing it wrong."

By focusing on your lack of technical expertise or inexperience, skeptics are likely to raise questions in the minds of other people about your ability to lead the effort. By making such blatant accusations, your critics will allow others to doubt the viability of the initiative: "Jane has been here only six months. She's not going to get the support from senior management for her idea. They don't know who she is." Or, "Jerry's field is computers. What does he know about accounting? He can't determine which financial software is best for us." By raising doubt in other people's minds, skeptics can mount a very effective attack against an initiative.

Another challenge you may face has to do with execution. In this instance, your objective may be above reproach, but to your critics, the process for implementing the planned action is flawed: "You should not have moved the computer center to the third floor in one full move. It should have been phased in." Or, "He's a horrible manager. Remember that last project? His indecision almost created a war around here. Can't the guy be clear about anything?"

While criticism may not be as open or explicit as this, you've heard similar comments about people who try to get something done in your organization. In these situations, critics put your initiative in jeopardy by questioning your ability to implement it.

Put another way, think about how many times you've read something like this in newspaper or magazine accounts of the ouster of an executive: "We agreed on the direction we wanted for the company, but we had differences of opinion over how to get there." That's a polite way of saying that they're "doing it all wrong."

Like the you-don't-know-the-issues-well-enough case, the you're-doing-it-wrong argument doesn't directly attack or oppose the idea. Instead, it tries to derail the effort by derailing the leader of the effort. Often, this argument strategy is employed when the leader has a notable weakness or vulnerability.

Consider a merger situation. There is a lot of jockeying for position and usually half the people are relatively unknown to their new colleagues. As merger integration or unit restructuring efforts get off the ground—common practice following a merger—the you're-doing-it-wrong arguments will be invoked frequently. Critics will point out how the people trying to lead the merger are not following an approach that will work with one of the merged entities or that the person leading the merger does not have the ability to implement the initiative successfully.

∾

Nathan Klein, the distribution manager at Sobel Wines, also had definite thoughts about the direction Troy was heading. Nathan liked the idea of expanding the business, because expansion would mean that he'd be able to wield more influence since he was in charge of the logistics of distribution. But Nathan wasn't behind Troy 100 percent. He thought they needed to focus more on getting the logistics right first and then finding the right suppliers. "Troy, I've been thinking about what you are proposing, but I think I have a problem with your approach. If we go out to potential suppliers of upscale wines without having our own house in order, we may end up with a situation where we can't deliver. What we need to do is a wall-to-wall assessment of our distribution systems and processes and identify what technologies we'll need, the cost, and how we may need to change our processes. Then, we can pursue vendors. Your approach is really putting the cart before the horse."

Common objection #6:
"You have ulterior motives."

Whenever you try to make something happen in an organization, there is a tendency to question the idea or the initiative. Ideas are never "pure." It is easy to dismiss anyone with an idea as having ulterior motives because there can be some pork in there somewhere. Anyone can attack you for having self-serving ulterior motives.

You've probably been on both sides of this situation. When one of your colleagues tries to make a change, one of your first thoughts may be something like, "Oh, he's just doing that so that he looks good to the executive vice president," or "He just wants to take over that department's activities." Or, "Don't think for a minute that he thinks we'll actually lose our competitive advantage. He just wants to take over the marketing department." The reasoning behind such challenges goes like this: "Why would anyone want to disrupt the status quo? They must have a reason."

In our post-Enron world, questions of motive, intention, and morality may be raised before questions of strategy, the value of the idea, or its viability. Distrust in organizations seems to be at an all-time high and no one is immune from criticism. Given the complexity of issues and actions that people routinely deal with, it is relatively easy for a detractor to find inconsistent or conflicting actions by those leading new initiatives.

You need to be ready to face questions regarding your motives and intentions. No matter how complete your response, no matter how well prepared you are to refute accusations, you can be sure that arguments against your idea will persist. If you aren't careful, every action you take will be placed under a microscope and analyzed by your detractors to somehow expose you as . . . that's right . . . a Machiavellian schemer!

&

Frank Russo, Sobel Wines's financial guru, was also skeptical. Frank, one of the few nonfamily members in senior management, never liked the fact that an outsider became his boss. When it was Frank's turn to speak, he said, "Troy, I know there's been a lot of pressure on you to grow the business. But I think you're starting to create initiatives that buy you time to figure something else out. You don't really think this program can work, do you? If you need more time to develop a plan that can work, just say so, Troy. But don't take us on a wild-goose chase just to give you time to think!"

๑

Every time you make a suggestion, someone will make at least one of the six arguments mentioned or a variation:

- "Your idea is too risky."
- "That idea will actually make things worse."
- "Your proposal won't change a thing."
- "You don't know the issues well enough."
- "You're doing it wrong."
- "You have ulterior motives."

le projet

la personne

Think of an example from everyday life. You've lived in Manhattan for fifteen years and have now decided that the time has come to move north to the suburbs in Dutchess County. The schools are better. You can get a little land. You can spend more time outdoors, so on and so forth.

"Right," says your wife. "We have absolutely no idea what the consequences of moving to that place will be. We don't know what the schools are like. We certainly don't know what the quality of life is like up there at all. I have no idea what a deer tick looks like, and God knows I wouldn't know a lime from Lyme disease."

You respond by maintaining that given a little time the risks will be clear.

Now your son reacts by telling you that not only is it risky, but it will make things worse. "Dad, you are hardly at home. This means that you will be commuting three hours a day. We will have to buy another car. We would never spend any time together, even if we did have a backyard. How do you know that kids upstate have fewer drug problems than kids here? At least here, I know I can handle it. It is just going to make things worse."

Finally, your parents, who live next door, get in on the act. Your mother says, "This isn't going to change a thing. Whatever problems you have, you will move them with you. Maybe you'll even get new headaches to substitute for the old ones. Life on 86th Street isn't that bad. You can go visit Dutchess County. Dad has a fishing pole you can borrow."

Whether you are working in a corporation, a union, a school, or a government agency or whether you are a manager, a social worker, a schoolteacher, or a politician, it is inevitable that whenever you want to take action people will challenge your ideas because your ideas infringe on their notions of what should or should not be done. Inertia is the most comfortable state. When you come in to propose an alternative, what do you really expect? Do you think that they will wrap their arms around you and accept you with all your messianic zeal, as if this is exactly what they were waiting for? Even if they don't challenge your idea—or if they are neutral—there is a good chance that they will take some digs at you and question your knowledge, your ability, and your motivation.

You can protect yourself and your ideas from veiled or outright attacks. The basic reaction to a challenge to your idea is to delegitimize your challenger. This can be accomplished in three ways. The first is confrontation: Take their argument head on, point by point, to show that their reasoning is fallacious or inaccurate. The second way of delegitimizing your opponents is to let them rant and rave, let them exhaust themselves and their ideas through repetition. Finally, you can go around them. Delegitimize them by making your case to their peers, colleagues, and supervisors. The problem with each of these delegitimizing efforts is that they are defensive actions and are likely to create antagonism.

Political competence requires that you take into account the agendas of others. Rather than react by undercutting your critics, you begin to think how you can pull them in. You need to think about how you can adjust the situation to your advantage to strengthen alliances and co-opt the opposition. Therefore, the first step is to understand how others think and what their agendas are.

Chapter 2

Analyze Goals and Approaches

You know you face skeptics. They've argued that your idea is too risky, that it will make things worse, that it won't change a thing, and they have questioned your methods, your knowledge, and your motives. Your challenge now is to understand them. How do you size them up? How do you figure out where others in the organization are coming from? Few people will tell you directly that they are against taking any sort of action.*

---

* Many of the categories used in this chapter originated from a series of interviews of school administrators and teachers regarding efforts at implementing education reform. It became clear that individuals, at all levels of the school district, operate differently in terms of goals and style. In a number of seminars, I found that the particular categories used here work well in letting individuals identify the approach others in the organization take. These categories also work in the public sector, high-tech organizations, hospitals, manufacturing, etc. This leads me to believe that they are not specific to any one type of organization.

Nearly everyone presents a veneer of being proactive, even if they intend to take no action at all. Nowadays, conflict is rarely between those who resist change and those who advocate change, but almost always over the agendas for change that people have. No one is going to come out and say, "Things are great as they are and I am against any change." Instead they will say, "Let's wait. We have time to take action." Or, "We need to take a different type of action."

Think about the people you work with. Ask yourself: *What are their goals?* In trying to understand the goals of others, you should ask: *What are their goals; that is, what is the scope of their purpose or the ends that they want to pursue?* Their goals may be understood on a continuum from tinkering to overhauling.

You need to differentiate between individuals with *tinkering goals*—very narrow and well-defined change objectives—versus those with *overhauling goals*—broader change objectives. Tinkerers pursue narrow ends while overhaulers pursue broader ends.

The Tinkering Approach

Tinkering goals tend to be incremental improvements in the status quo of the organization. The changes a tinkerer makes are first-order changes that do not fundamentally transform the organization. Tinkerers are concerned about changes in specific rules and operations and tend to be risk-averse.

You know tinkerers. They are careful. They look like they are merely shuffling papers on their desk, but they are not.

They are making changes that are specific, defined, and contained. Tinkerers make a list and prioritize which item they should pursue first. *We are going to concentrate on improving our communication system and here's what we are going to do about it.* Tinkerers are focused on the short term, constantly thinking of the specific things they can do immediately.

Instead of aiming at major transformation, tinkerers target opportunities to achieve operational efficiencies. They would rather expand business in a geographic region that they already serve or seek out customers who are similar to the ones they already work with than tap new markets or implement a thoroughly new way of doing business.

Often, tinkerers will focus on improving communication flow, upgrading problem-solving mechanisms, or enhancing the quality of products and services. For tinkerers, the risk associated with their methods is fairly low. They prefer doing things the unit has already done before—just doing them a little bit better, a little bit more frequently, a little bit faster, or a little bit more cost-effectively. They redecorate, redesign, and re-engineer. While tinkering may have negative connotations, organizational tinkerers have their place. Tinkering goals work best during stable times—when the fundamentals of the organization are in good shape. All of the tinkerer's activity is within the framework of making specific, incremental improvements.

The tinkerer is most likely to fail when a business really requires a new way of doing things. In the disk drive industry, you can imagine the manufacturers of 5.25-inch drives justifying a few incremental improvements that would continue to provide market dominance over those upstart 3.5-inch drive makers, when they could have been rethinking their product line completely in an attempt to jump ahead with a superior product. The manufacturers of the 5.25-inch drives were tinkerers when tinkering was detrimental to their firms' very existence. (This example can be found in Clayton Christensen's book *The Innovator's Dilemma* [HarperBusiness, 2003].)

Take the example of an executive education program at a prestigious academic institution under the directorship of a tinkerer. For years, the program rested comfortably and profitably on the reputation of the degree-granting division of the university, and offered a popular training program for executives. Then, in the mid-1990s, a number of competing programs came on the market. A few universities in the same geographic region began offering their own brand of executive education. More corporations tried their hand at offering high-level training in-house. New organizations, not tied to academic institutions, emerged to provide programs dedicated to quality executive education. Some courses were offered online, eliminating the need for a classroom or the physical presence of an instructor.

The head of the executive education program responded to the challenge with incremental, tactical adjustments, preferring to tweak course content and change the structure of the organization. It was not a good time to have a tinkerer at the helm.

The same contrast between tinkering and overhauling can happen in a marriage. Together, you rotate schedules, shift responsibilities, and work on your communication. But while she wants to talk about the garbage and deal with schedules for taking the kids to school, you want to go to a four-day gestalt couples retreat in the Adirondacks for a period of reflection and overhaul.

For certain people, tinkering goals are not enough: They have broader ambitions, more encompassing ends. They want to move beyond first-order change to the bigger questions: commitment, love, products, war, peace, the definition of profit—such agents of change are more interested in overhauling.

The Overhauling Approach

To continue the story of the struggling executive education program, the directors—those who developed the curriculum and course content—were not satisfied with the tinkering approach when they saw enrollments and profits decrease due to competition. They wanted to strip down the program and rebuild with a fresh focus—a focus that met the demands of their prospective students. Their method was not one of tinkering; rather, it was one of *overhauling*.*

---

* For a discussion of this concept in a nonorganizational setting, see Thomas S. Kuhn's classical distinction between those who would tinker within a paradigm and those who would overhaul a paradigm, as discussed in his book *The Structure of Scientific Revolutions* (University of Chicago Press, 1962).

Overhaulers are not so much concerned with incremental changes as with broader goals. What interests them is not the rules and operations but the underlying motivation. You know overhaulers. They tell you: "We should be in a different place." Or, "We should be moving in a different direction." They are perpetually looking under the surface. If the tinkerer is slow and incremental and makes focused adjustments, the overhauler is rapid and broad and sometimes throws out the baby with the bathwater.

The overhauler is intent on putting the unit on a new trajectory. Instead of eking out a percentage improvement here, or a slightly lower cost structure there, they look for fundamental transformation and, in the process, a dramatic retooling of what their unit does.

Consider the American economy over the last several years. In the conference rooms of any large corporation in 1997 you were likely to hear cries for overhaul: "We need to be more like an Internet company." "E-business is our future." "If we don't change our business model, we may not exist in five years." People were talking about a no-holds-barred approach to making business decisions and implementing changes in their environment.

Fast-forward to 2002. In those same conference rooms—assuming the company hasn't left that office space after being downsized—you'll likely hear pleas of: "We need to work smarter." "Our budget's been slashed 15 percent across the board, so we need to find areas where we can cut costs." "We're considering expanding our marketing efforts beyond the metropolitan area and into upstate New York." These are still the voices of overhaulers, but instead of looking for the unanticipated, they are advocating bringing the organization "back to basics."

Tinkerers say to Overhaulers	Overhaulers say to Tinkerers
You are moving too fast!	*You are moving too slow!*
You are panicking— there are no icebergs!	*We're on the Titanic and you're rearranging the deck chairs!*
You underestimate our strengths.	*You are ignoring the realities of our market.*

Figure Out the Approach of Others

Just as individuals differ in the goals they want to pursue, they also differ in the approach or means by which they intend to achieve those ends. Some individuals want to attain narrow, specific, tinkering goals, while others seek broad, general, overhauling objectives. They will also differ in the means they will use to pursue these goals.

Often, shared understanding in an organization may simply be the shared understanding of the end game. Rarely, if ever, is there a shared understanding or an agreement about how the organization should achieve its goals.

To go back to our marriage example, your wife realizes that just discussing the garbage may not be enough, that she may have to compromise with you—tinkering will not save the day. Indeed, you may need to discuss your notion of love, and a little overhaul may be in order. But she's done her research. She has spoken to six different therapists, and she has concluded that the gestalt approach is not for her. She decides that the two of you need to see a family-systems expert for fourteen sessions at $135 a session. You, on the other hand, want to go on a retreat and see what happens—take it one step at a time.

Basically the two of you have different management approaches. She believes in planning, you in improvising.

The Planning Approach

Those who take the planning approach assume that individuals can minimize the risk of a meteor hitting the organization by consolidating and focusing on systems of accountability. Planners believe that everything that affects us can be known and prepared for, and that they can identify all of the issues, problems, and variables in order to estimate, with some accuracy, the likely outcomes and consequences of their decisions.

In the mind of the planner, relationships between current conditions and future circumstances are, for the most part, linear and predictable. In other words, everything can be accounted for and survival is a matter of collecting information, ensuring the accuracy of facts, and estimating with more skill than one's competitors.

In a situation full of ambiguity and uncertainty, adopting a planning approach minimizes flexibility and narrows the number of decisions. Planners are most concerned with control, a high level of interdependence (knowing what is being done by whom), regimen (consistency in what is being done), and accountability (who reports to whom). Planners want to calculate change, harmonize activities, and synchronize the various components of the organization. Individuals with this approach want to segment functions and control actions in order to be as productive as possible. That is, their goal is to maximize the efficiency of their deliberate actions.

In organizations dominated by a planning approach, individuals have well-defined roles and responsibilities. Each action can be judged by precedent and by goals, which are often clearly stated. A clear framework decreases ambiguity and vulnerability, in terms of the organization's production and its members' productivity. Planners believe in the beauty and coherence of the plan and rely on the numbers to "prove" the plan will succeed.

Consider a fire department. Fire departments have many planners who lay out very specific plans and actions to take for a wide range of situations. Of course, each fire situation is different—requiring real-time thinking and spontaneous action. But, for the most part, there is a structured approach and protocol for fighting fires.

Fire department leaders have created specific procedures and actions for responding to a fire in an apartment building.

When arriving on the scene, firefighters have a relatively clear set of tasks that they need to follow. They do not improvise— that would result in chaos and, perhaps, fatalities. Instead, fire chiefs have gone through planning with their company and have reviewed and tested specific procedures that the firefighters in the company know to follow.

Fire units specializing in fighting California forest fires are well trained for their jobs. You would not expect a New York City firefighter to immediately know how to manage a blaze in a forest. There are clearly defined procedures, well-articulated roles and responsibilities, and there should be very few sur- prises when a firefighter comes onto the scene—in a wooded or an urban area. Units for fighting fires and firefighters are good examples of organizations and individuals who operate well with a planning approach.

A planning approach is based on the optimistic assumption that—within acceptable probabilities—the future can be pre- dicted and, more importantly, controlled.

Your wife thinks that if you two find the right therapist, one whose talent matches the problem and who will listen carefully, you, as a couple, will be able to reconstitute the fun- damentals of your marriage. Planners are not experiential. They do not live in the moment, and, indeed, they are true believers in their ability to anticipate.

You may believe that the future is unpredictable, that orga- nizations are perpetually messy, and that there are too many conflicting forces that disrupt any kind of clarity in organiza- tions. Planners are often criticized for being overly concerned about making the present and the future match—trying to balance two imaginary worlds. And, too often, planners end up oversimplifying the conditions they're operating under.

So, you tell your wife that you can't plan your way back to happiness. But you simply have to "live" your way back to happiness through daily improvisation—one moment at a time.

The Improvising Approach

Improvisation, as an approach, is based on the assumption that individuals can minimize the risk of a meteor hitting by building flexibility into the system. They assume that they "can't see around the corner." Knowing they can't see around the corner, they don't make concrete plans, but rather react as events unfold. Uncertainty of markets, politics, indeed the uncertainty of life has made it more difficult to anticipate and to plan. Improvisers are prepared for and skilled in creative, fluid adaptation.

Improvisers are obsessed with perpetual adaptability. They try to minimize risk by looking at what others are doing, by acting and then reassessing. Improvisers believe that because no one can accurately predict the future, it is necessary to proceed by trial and error. Act first and see what works. In other words, learn from your experience and from what others are doing.

Improvisers attempt to imitate the successes and avoid the failures of others. They often operate on the basis of experience, values, and norms, rather than on abstract or logical calculations.

They rely heavily on their own and on others' practical experience. For this reason, individuals with an improvisational approach are concerned with autonomy, a high level of independence (letting people figure out what they need to do), openness and flexibility (allowing for a variety of methods), and personal responsibility. Improvisers feel that people have to learn through experience.

During tight economic times, improvisers often don't have the necessary discipline, and this makes improvisation strategies less advantageous. Start-up entrepreneurs are classic improvisers. During the Internet boom of the 1990s, these improvisers shaked and baked through turbulent growth and relied on their adaptive ability to seek opportunities, react to ineffective business models, and make the midcourse corrections—and their firms became the darlings of management magazines around the world. During the severe business retraction from 1999 through 2003, improvisers found their bob-and-weave approach hopelessly inadequate when they had to stop the bleeding from their collapsing ventures. Numerous firms closed their doors as a result of their reliance on inadequate business models and their seat-of-the-pants approach to change.

◈

Dan Gillespie walked into his boss's office like a puppy bringing back a bone from the woods. Dan was a salesperson for a computer software company, and he had an idea for a great new incentive program to offer to customers. Dan's boss,

Pat Browe, listened eagerly and responded, "That's brilliant. Let's put a quick presentation together; we'll run through some numbers, have a discussion with marketing, and bring it up at the next sales meeting for feedback and reactions. I think you're really onto something here."

Dan's face had dropped about three stories before he could finally speak, "Pat, you don't understand; we've got to run with this now. If we wait too long and have meetings and all that other stuff, we'll miss the opportunity I have. The Freestone Fruit account is in a position to really push our stuff. If I don't get them over the top by next week, they'll get excited about someone else's software. That's just how things work at that chain."

"I appreciate that, Dan. But if other retailers or others on our sales staff hear about your incentive program, they'll be irate that they weren't informed about it. We'll have a lot of chaos around here."

"That'll blow over when they start to see the results. They'll forget they even had a problem with this! Listen, we can talk about it all day and we can look at numbers. But the bottom line is that until we try it out, we'll never know what kind of potential it has. If I didn't have an excited customer nipping at my heels as we speak, I'd never try to push it through so quickly. But we've gotta be able to pursue these kinds of opportunities."

"I understand what you're saying, Dan. And I'm the last person who wants to limit our growth potential. But I have to believe there are some issues we haven't thought about yet."

"Let's just try it. I'll keep it low-key and under wraps. But let's move forward and see what happens. In the worst case, the program won't work and then no one will be talking about it or they'll be happy that they didn't know about it. Please don't stonewall me on this one."

∽

The improvisational approach is ideal for making rapid adjustments. It is great for innovation. It is strong for seeing new opportunities, anticipating new options, and expecting the unexpected.

The weakness of an improvisational approach is that too much extemporaneous action can take organizations off-course. By constantly adapting to change, the organization can

Planners say to Improvisers	Improvisers say to Planners
You are just pursuing the idea du jour!	*You are missing a huge opportunity.*
You are out of control!	*You're cutting off options!*
Where is your detailed plan?	*What happens if things don't go as planned?*
Logistics is everything.	*Let's move!*

lose sight of its goals. Another drawback is that improvisation can be costly and efforts are more likely to grow out of control.

How do you want to put change in place? Do you want to operate as a planner or as an improviser? In the past, most of the world operated in a planning mode. People would make plans for their careers, for a particular marketing strategy, for corporations and governments. This linear model was ingrained into the practices of most organizations. In reality, you sometimes plan, but what you really do is bob and weave. We now live in an organizational world where improvising is inevitable. Even as you plan, you've got to constantly make adjustments.

The politically competent decide when it is appropriate to plan and when it is appropriate to improvise. Planning may be appropriate in terms of the medium and long run. But in the short run, to make planning work, you're going to have to improvise. To have planning without improvising is to create rigidity and doom your change effort to failure. To improvise without planning is to create chaos that will derail your effort.

In the next chapter, you'll see that analyzing the goals and approaches of others will help you decipher their agenda. Agendas have two components: What people want to achieve and how they want to achieve it. Analyzing the goals and approaches of others is a way of getting a handle on their agendas.

Chapter 3

Understand the Agendas

You want to push an idea and get something done. But maybe your colleagues think that you're being too conservative and that you should overhaul the entire mission of the department. Others think that you're being too radical and that you should just tinker a little by rewriting some job descriptions. Maybe some in the organization would prefer that you deal with this issue in an ad hoc manner, making informal adjustments as you go along, while others would prefer that you be very formal and explicit in terms of where you want to move the division.

In order to understand who is likely to support you and who is not, you have to ask yourself:

1. What are the goals of others—tinkering or overhauling?
2. What are the approaches of others—improvising or planning?

With the answers to these questions, you will be able to categorize the agendas of your colleagues and yourself into one of four types: *Traditionalist, Adjuster, Developer,* and *Revolutionary.* With this, you will begin to understand how their agenda compares to yours. These agendas tell you in what ways your approach to any given problem is similar to and different from others' approaches to the same problem. When you understand those differences, you'll be better equipped to identify how to bring your colleagues on board—and how to identify the ones who may *never* come on board.

In today's organizations, the real conflict is not between those who resist change and those who advocate change. Conflict is over the change agenda. Therefore, political competence demands that you analyze and understand the agendas of others in order to anticipate how they will react to your efforts.

Below is a graphical representation of the four agendas as they relate to goals and approaches:

	Tinkering Goals	Overhauling Goals
Planning Approach	Traditionalist Agenda	Developer Agenda
Improvising Approach	Adjuster Agenda	Revolutionary Agenda

The Traditionalist Agenda

As you can see from the diagram, by choosing a Traditionalist agenda, you combine the goals of tinkering with a planning approach. Traditionalist agendas, while not against new ideas *per se,* are leery of them. The rhetoric of the Traditionalist agenda is that change should be regenerative—that its purpose is to integrate the past successes of the organization into its current reality.*

Traditionalist agendas treat the current problems in the organization as a breakdown of tradition. Any change initiative should focus on getting back on track—in some sense—returning to the old ways. If you adopt a Traditionalist agenda, you will likely argue that once-abandoned routines are the best way to deal with uncertain and ambiguous environments.

Traditionalist agendas link similarities between past problems, hazards, constraints, and opportunities with those that the organization faces today and will face tomorrow. This agenda implies a cyclical approach to change: History does indeed repeat itself. Managers choosing Traditionalist agendas

---

* There have been many attempts to identify actors involved in change. James MacGregor Burns, in his work on FDR (*Transforming Leadership,* Atlantic Monthly Press, 2003), distinguishes between the inheritors, innovators, opposers, partners, coalition builders, splitters, passives, and isolates. Each plays a role—positive, negative, or neutral—in any change effort. Burns applies these terms in a public policy setting, but in doing so, shows the appropriateness of these categories to all organizational settings.

often use romanticized language to express their position. The Traditionalist agenda is much more focused on tinkering than on overhauling.

The strength of the Traditionalist agenda is its cautiousness, its reflective approach, and its ability to draw on the visible experience of the past to support current positions. This agenda's weakness is its focus on the past—to the point that it ignores important differences between the past and the present situation. Also, depending on the circumstances, a Traditionalist agenda may be an overly conservative position, causing the organization to miss important opportunities. When conceding to change, those who choose a Traditionalist agenda prefer to build time into the process, feeling that the longer the process takes, the more constrained the change will be and the greater their control will be.

Walter B. Hewlett would be considered to have had a Traditionalist agenda, in regard to Hewlett-Packard's decision to merge with Compaq. He was the only board member who continued to oppose HP's merger with Compaq, even after the merger took place. Hewlett felt the merger would cause HP to sprawl into the low-profit PC market, thus hurting HP's crown jewel—the printer business.

Hewlett insisted that he was not opposed to change *per se*, but rather that he disagreed with the merger strategy, which reflected a company-wide shift from one of "focus" to one of "scale." Hewlett stated that ". . . the fundamental mistake in the thinking behind the merger was the perceived need to do something with scale, instead of succeeding the way HP has in the past, with focus and innovation."* Hewlett's opponents argued that today's turbulent environment required that HP become a "full service supplier of hardware, software, and services to large corporate customers,"** along the lines of IBM. This could only be achieved through the merger, which would allow HP to consolidate PC operations with Compaq and that the new enterprise would dominate the PC market. From this perspective, Hewlett's Traditionalist rhetoric was seen as being overly constraining and insensitive to the reality of the current business environment.

Hewlett was strongly criticized by some for being too resistant to change. Supporters, on the other hand, including stock analysts, investors, and strategists, thought Hewlett's perspective was right on the mark and exactly what HP needed during a volatile time.

Those choosing a Traditionalist agenda are not restricted to the corporate world. One of the problems in academia, especially at research universities, is determining the best way to spread responsibility and rewards among faculty members, who have two primary functions: to conduct research and to teach. Recently a colleague burst into my office with a great new idea. He suggested that researchers with large grants do less teaching, while faculty members who publish less should

---

* As quoted in Steve Lohr's article "Technology; Hewlett Heir Issues Letter Denouncing Planned Deal," *The New York Times,* December 14, 2001.
** As quoted in Lohr's article, "Technology Briefing Software: Endorsement for Hewlett Deal," *The New York Times,* January 29, 2002.

do more teaching. He thought it would balance the equation of effort and reward.

I remembered when I first heard this idea in 1974 and the faculty raised hell. I told my young colleague that the very idea he was proposing was on a certain level an anathema to the cherished traditions of the college. The administration's strength has always been its willingness to be flexible and allow faculty members to choose the direction that they preferred. I reminisced about the old days when we were a small faculty and everyone was motivated by a sense of community to do research and to take pride in their teaching. I liked things the way they were. In those days, I told my colleague, "We didn't motivate by making promises; we motivated people by socializing them, by ingraining them with a sense of what it means to be an academic. And today, everything is tit-for-tat—if I do this, what will I get in return?"

My colleague was right when he said we needed to make some changes, but my preference was to recreate that old sense of community rather that throw my weight behind a radical change. Notice my reaction: I wasn't being obstructionist; I wasn't against change. But I was resisting it mildly. With my greater experience, I recalled for my colleague a history of which he was unaware. My Traditionalist rhetorical strategy was not to stop him from embarking on his change initiative, but to slow him down a little bit.

The Traditionalist agenda has the advantage of controlling what may be impulsive action, while having the disadvantage of constraining spontaneity. Therefore, in trying to take some action and pushing your ideas, you have to consider that there are advantages and disadvantages in having the support of a Traditionalist agenda. The advantage is that the person choosing a Traditionalist agenda will constantly take you back to the historical context in which you are taking action. He or she will point out, "We've been here before," and will try to anchor you in inertia. Adopting a Traditionalist agenda usually involves telling anecdotes of parallel historical situations. The disadvantage is that, if you adopt the agenda of a Traditionalist, you may be seen as being too conservative. The issue for you will be how to gain the support of those with Traditionalist agendas without falling prey to their inclination toward inertia.

The Adjuster Agenda

If you adopt an Adjuster agenda, you assume that change is natural, inevitable, and unpredictable; and you will likely react only when necessary. Unlike the Traditionalist agenda, which draws inspiration from the past, an Adjuster agenda is very much in the present and is responsive to external circumstances. If you choose an Adjuster agenda, you constantly re-assimilate yourself into the changing environment. The rhetorical image of the Adjuster agenda is one of ebb and flow, of rolling with the punches. The merger and acquisitions lawyer who repackages himself as a bankruptcy and reorganization specialist when the economy tanks has adopted an Adjuster agenda.

As you can see from the position on the previous chart, those choosing an Adjuster agenda are usually more comfortable making tinkering changes and improvising as they go along, crossing that bridge when they get to it. The person pursuing an Adjuster agenda monitors the environment and tries to isolate those factors that demand action. They act only when there is an absolute necessity to adapt.

A securities broker, pursuing a classic Adjuster agenda, may say, "In a bear market, we sell bonds and security. In a bull market, we sell risk and equity. Look at what the customer needs, help the customer find it, and make the appropriate adjustment. Move your product with your customer. Know when the time has come to make an adjustment."

In a bear market, turnover of money slows. Customers are less likely to move from one bond to another as quickly as they would move from one stock to another. Therefore, in a bear market, structural adjustments are typical, consolidation occurs, and layoffs are rampant. This does not happen with the idea of fundamentally changing the organization. Rather, this is done in the spirit of making adjustments, of constantly evaluating and reacting.

The question for the manager pursuing an Adjuster agenda is one of timing—*when* to make the adjustment, *when* to expand, *when* to consolidate, and *when* to adapt—and determining just *when* has the bridge been approached. A manager pursuing an Adjuster agenda will anticipate oncoming environmental pressure but will not jump the gun. He will move just when he has to.

Consider the career of one marketing manager at a global fast-food chain. For years, his company offered only hamburgers on their menu. During the late 1970s, though, American tastes changed and health concerns increased. By the 1980s a few competitors expanded their menus to include chicken. In response, the marketing manager of the global chain pushed for—and introduced—a line of products featuring chicken. In the new century, tastes and attitudes underwent another transformation. Nutritional concerns escalated and more Americans began to pursue low-carb, low-fat diets. Salad bars and other healthy alternatives made their way onto the menus of competitors. The marketing manager made another adjustment—he began to push for the introduction of salads to the fast-food menu. The marketing manager never broke the new ground for the industry. His moves were measured and driven, to a large extent, by what McDonald's or Burger King did. He used the moves of others to justify and validate the moves he chose on behalf of his organization. These are the political and strategic activities of an Adjuster agenda.

IBM almost missed the growth in the PC market. (For a full discussion of this story, see D. Quinn Mills and G. Bruce Friesen's book *Broken Promises: An Unconventional View of What Went Wrong at IBM* [Harvard Business School Press, 1996].) With a strong corps of staff pursuing Traditionalist agendas, who urged the firm to "stick to its knitting" of mainframes and mini-computers, IBM showed up very late to the PC party. The Adjuster agendas' viewpoint gained legitimacy when large corporate customers started to ask IBM for PCs. It wasn't long after getting into the market that the PC industry boomed—first in the corporate sector and then with the household market for personal computers.

Adjuster agendas tend to be strongly influenced by externally driven factors and are more likely to be reactionary than proactive. Those pursuing an Adjuster agenda, as such, will come along with you on a new idea, but you are going to have to persuade them that it's time to cross the bridge. Unlike adopting a Traditionalist agenda, adopting an Adjuster agenda will rarely hold you back. But it may not push you forward. Think of Adjuster agendas as cautious but active.

The Developer Agenda

When you choose a Developer agenda, you are committed to staying on top of things—empirically, rationally, and incrementally. As a combination of a planning and overhauling, those choosing a Developer agenda will help you to formalize, codify, and quantify the change process. The rhetoric of the developer agenda is one of operational proficiency. If you adopt a Developer agenda, you will likely believe that a scientific or systematic method is essential for predicting and controlling impending change. You will want to gather information, scientific data, and analyses as well as clearly delineate each step of the way.

Those choosing Developer agendas believe that if the end goal can be defined, the steps needed to get there can be broken down into specific elements and reconstituted into a policy and a plan for organizational change. When working in an ambiguous environment, the person pursuing a Developer agenda will clearly try to create a plan.

Their strength is their ability to deal with change through studied anticipation. The weakness of choosing a Developer agenda is that you may overplan and box yourself into pursuing objectives that over the course of time may become obsolete. Developer agendas often have ambitious overhauling goals, but pursue them in a methodical and plodding manner.

Six Sigma, the quality improvement method first used effectively at Motorola—then at GE, Honeywell, and others—offers a good example of a Developer agenda at work. Six Sigma efforts start with a mandate for overhauling a specific set of business processes.* Jack Welch launched the Six Sigma effort at GE by famously describing its management as having ". . . its face to the CEO and its ass to the customer."** In other words, Welch called for total overhaul of the way GE thought about customer satisfaction—and in a way that would require changing the way GE manufactured, distributed, and sold their products and services.

---

* For a discussion of this concept, see James Biolos's article "Six Sigma Meets the Service Economy," *Harvard Management Update,* November 1, 2002.

** As quoted in Jerry Ussam's article "The Embattled CEO: Tyrants, Statesmen, and Destroyers (A Brief History of the CEO)," *Fortune,* November 18, 2002.

Though the objective of Six Sigma is one of dramatic overhaul, its method for achieving its goal is anything but radical. Its management approach is highly structured, using measuring, mapping, and redesigning processes that rely heavily on statistical analysis and, depending on which Six Sigma model is used, a dozen standard steps toward effective implementation. It is this type of planning, structure, and process that brings a tear of joy to a Developer's eye.

Those pursuing a Developer agenda love change initiatives, like Six Sigma, because of their structure. The inputs and outputs are knowable and quantifiable. The approach is broken down into discrete components that can be measured along specific criteria. Its strength comes from an organization's ability to prepare.

The problem, though, with many Six Sigma efforts—and initiatives like it—is that despite all of their promise, they don't account for the human relationships and cultural issues that figure prominently in the success—and failure—of those efforts.

Even though those pursuing Developer agendas have broad ambitions, they often travel along a narrow path, thereby undoing the very goal to which they are committed. Developer agendas are very proactive in the pursuit of an agenda to which they feel ownership. They will run with a specific idea that they see as critical. The advantage of choosing people with a Developer agenda in your coalition is that their conviction can bring momentum to your effort. However, trouble can brew when that same conviction makes it difficult for you to deal with them if you veer from the specifics.

The Revolutionary Agenda

Unlike those pursuing a Developer agenda, and certainly unlike Adjuster agendas, Revolutionary agendas do NOT seek the implementation of a few novel ideas. Their goal, instead, is to impose a completely new set of ideas that will fundamentally transform the mission and the processes of the organization. Those with a Revolutionary agenda keenly believe that over-throwing the current way of doing business is crucial to the health of the organization. They deal with change in terms of radical action.

Revolutionaries thrive on new ideas and new twists on old ideas. Always looking to push the envelope, Revolutionaries are likely to focus on new technologies, emerging markets, and up-to-the-minute research as the impetus for change.

Like Developer agendas, Revolutionary agendas seek to overhaul their units or organizations. Unlike those choosing a Developer agenda—who won't engage in overhauling until a well-constructed plan is in place—Revolutionaries don't develop well-constructed plans. In order to respond to subtle changes in the environment, they improvise.

While pursuing a Revolutionary agenda often entails the most risk, it also enables you to be nimble and reactive—shifting direction or re-evaluating your situation more easily than if you invested heavily in structured plans.

A Revolutionary agenda implies that you regard incre-mental change as something of a distraction. In other words, why make minor changes here and there when, over the long term, the organization will likely need to be in a fundamentally new place? For those pursuing a Revolutionary agenda, focusing on incremental improvements sidetracks an organization from its long-term goals and keeps everyone in a rut.

Imagine that you are an engineer working at a large conglomerate in the early 1960s. At the time, your company had three core businesses: forestry products, rubber products, and a cable works. But you've been dreaming about—and begun developing—an esoteric piece of electronics that would analyze performance in nuclear power plants. So you go to your boss and say something like, "All right, I *know* we are in the paper business and the rubber business and the cable business. But I think we need to be in the electronics business." In most organizations, you'd be led out the front door quickly or, at best, you'd develop a reputation as frequently choosing Revolutionary agendas and be marginalized, stripped of a budget, and relegated to the rear parking lot.

However, your company has a long history of getting into new businesses. While you may have a Revolutionary agenda, you are fortunate enough to be operating in an organization that accommodates and nurtures Revolutionary ideas. You see your little pulse analyzer through the development process. Little did you know that your revolutionary foray would help to build an electronics business that would eventually lead to its global market leadership position in cell phones! Though not all stories about revolutionaries have the same happy ending, this story shows how revolutionaries challenge their organizations to think differently about what they do and how they do it.

The weakness of the Revolutionary agenda is that those who have it can be dreamers, and take the organization on some dangerous side trips, while never really arriving at any destination in particular. Another drawback is that you might quickly jump to the idea of the day rather than focus on agendas with clear long-term advantages.

The strength of a Revolutionary agenda is that it will perpetually push the organization toward its limits, but that can be a danger as well. When trying to get a person with a Revolutionary agenda to join your initiative, you should be aware that they can undermine your efforts. Just as a Traditionalist agenda can mire you in inertia, a Revolutionary agenda can lead you over the top. No matter what you say or do, there will be times that someone with a Revolutionary agenda will contend that you didn't go far enough.

Taking Stock

The minute you want to do something different in your organization, you will attract allies and repel skeptics. At that point, you are vulnerable to the arguments of others. Those arguments will take the form of critiques of your idea—the thing you want to get done. But resistance will also take the form of criticism targeting you and your capacity to be leading such an agenda. Keep in mind, these aren't necessarily attacks against you personally, but are methods people use to stop something that they think will leave them worse off than they are under the current conditions. So you need to prepare for arguments against your idea and against you.

One of the first ways to prepare for resistance is by understanding the mindsets of the people in your organization. You need to understand that resistance to your idea is largely about others seeing the world differently than you do. To prepare your defense—and offense—you need to understand the perspectives of others. If you can do that successfully, you will likely uncover ways to bring on more allies and to reduce the impact that terminal skeptics will have on your effort.

Different perspectives, as we've seen, fall into two broad categories:

1. Those with different goals (Tinkering and Overhauling)
2. Those with different implementation approaches (Planning and Improvising)

With careful preparation and analysis, you'll be able to understand to what degree key people in the organization share your goals and to what degree they share your approach.

And when you consider goals and approaches together, you'll find that people have one of four different possible agendas, as they relate to your initiative. They may choose Traditionalist agendas—wanting to keep things the same as much as possible. Or, they may have chosen an Adjuster agenda—people who are open to incremental changes. Developer agendas are open to more large-scale change, but only if it can be pursued in a very measured way. And, finally, there are Revolutionary agendas, which suggest that large-scale change has to happen and that the organization needs to move forward now before opportunities are lost.

Once you identify which agenda your initiative falls under, you can better identify the agendas that others have, relative to yours. And when you've mapped the agendas of others, you'll be prepared to take the next step in moving your agenda forward: building your coalition.

Chapter 4

Identify Allies and Resistors

So here you are. You know that you have to initiate some action, but you also know that your agenda will differ from the agendas of others in your organization.

On a particular issue, you may have a Revolutionary agenda, your supervisor has chosen a Traditionalist agenda, your colleague down the hall has a Developer agenda, and your assistant undoubtedly has an Adjuster agenda. You know that you cannot go it alone.

Now you must map the political terrain. That is, you must understand the agendas of others as they relate to your agenda in regard to a particular issue. If you're politically competent, you know you must complete this analysis of your organization's political environment before you can begin to effectively build support for your initiative. This involves the following four steps.

Step 1: Determine your agenda as it relates to your initiative. Is your agenda Traditionalist, Adjuster, Developer, or Revolutionary?

Step 2: List all the key stakeholders, as they relate to your initiative. Include those who may have competing objectives, as well as those who are key decision-makers, allies, and/or influencers.

Step 3: Identify the agenda of each stakeholder.

Step 4: Analyze that list, identifying those who are like you, those who are in opposite quadrants, and those who share either similar goals or similar implementation strategies.

Step 1: Determine What Kind of Agenda You Have

Keep in mind the matrix in the last chapter. You may intuitively know where your agenda falls. If you struggle in identifying your agenda, answer two sets of questions. First, consider your goals. *Are you after tinkering goals or overhauling goals? How would others describe you?* For the particular issue you are pushing, would you be seen as a tinkerer or an overhauler? While you may think your idea is radical, others may consider it only a small step toward the organization's goals. More commonly, particularly if you have a Revolutionary agenda, you may consider your initiative to be a baby step, while others think it is a giant leap into the dark!

Next, think about your management approach. *Are you an Improviser or a Planner?* Do you advocate developing a comprehensive, detailed plan before pursuing your initiative? Or are you more likely to deal with things as they come along and maintain that predicting accurately and acting incrementally is impossible?

Based on the answers to these two sets of questions, you should be able to place yourself in one of the four quadrants. Keep in mind that while you may choose a Revolutionary agenda for your initiative, you may choose a Traditionalist agenda for most other decisions in your organization. Agendas about change, well, change. So, don't assume. The CFO—normally pursuing a Revolutionary agenda—might choose an Adjuster agenda when it comes to your specific initiative. Always calibrate your stakeholders carefully for each issue as it arises.

§

George Irwin was assistant administrator at the Broome County Sisterhood Hospital in upstate New York, when the chief administrator called him in to ask him if he had an idea for making the hospital more efficient.

> *Administrator:* "We've grown so much. We need not only to become more efficient, but to think of the future—push the envelope, George."
>
> *George:* "Let's create satellite networks."
>
> *Administrator:* "What's a satellite network?"

George: "You know, little clinics spread through the region. We have some nurses there, we have some doctors there. We do preventive front-line medicine."

Administrator: "Preventive front-line medicine. I like the notion."

George is a Revolutionary with a great idea. He wants to develop small clinics, something that has been totally foreign to Broome County Sisterhood Hospital. His goal is one of over-hauling. His preferred approach—to move quickly in a sense-and-respond way—is the *modus operandi* of the Improviser. Once George understands his agenda is a Revolutionary one, he will be better prepared to compare his agenda with those of his colleagues.

Step 2: List the Key Stakeholders

List all the stakeholders. Stakeholders fall into four categories of people in organizations:

1. Decision-makers
2. Those who will be directly impacted by your initiative
3. Those at a similar level of influence in your organization, but who may not be directly impacted by your initiative (your colleagues)
4. Other influential stakeholders

Decision-makers are the top dogs and the ones who are ultimately responsible for the success of your initiative. The decision-maker may be an individual, like your boss, but more likely, decision-makers are a group, like senior management or the finance committee. They are the people who need to be on board and who will want to get a full perspective on your initiative before moving it forward. These are the people you will need to convince directly and who will heed the opinions of the other stakeholders in the organization.

Those who are directly impacted by your initiative will be, perhaps, your most challenging constituency. Within this group, you will find your most vocal detractors, including the detractors that you didn't even know about! This group will also have potential supporters. Do a careful job when developing a complete list of this group. It is often those on this level, who've been left out of the support-building process, who will become your harshest critics.

There is a cadre of *your colleagues* who share a similar level of influence in the organization. In most cases, they may not be significantly impacted by the change you are looking to effect. Nevertheless, everyone will undoubtedly have an opinion about what you are proposing and will have a measure of influence on the people who are making the ultimate decisions (or on those who will be directly impacted by your effort). Therefore, you'll need to list these people and, as best as you can, determine where they fall in the matrix.

Other stakeholders may include outside consultants, the board of directors, and people in the organization who might not fit into any of the above three categories, but who nevertheless have the attention of the decision-makers. Outside consultants inevitably become sounding boards for initiatives, and they are often influential in swaying the opinion of senior people. Sometimes, there are a few people who float at the periphery of the organization—such as a chief of staff for a senior person—who have the ability to weigh in with decision-makers on virtually any issue. Though this group may be difficult to identify and even more difficult to map accurately, just making yourself aware of their influence is an important step toward managing their influence.

The challenge is not simply to identify the high-profile stakeholders who will be impacted immediately, but also to identify the invisible stakeholders who will be impacted down the road. Political competence requires you to keep in mind that invisible stakeholders are not inactive stakeholders. The invisible stakeholders can be clients or vendors. They can be the marketing people who support the sales force. They can be in IT, training, or travel. Your invisible stakeholders can be at every level of the organization. You need to pay special attention to invisible stakeholders because they may become extremely active in resisting your idea. If the stakes are high enough, they will come out of the closet and become active resistors—or active supporters.

❧

George Irwin sat down at his desk and went over the organizational chart. He thought to himself, "Hmm. My boss, Harold Roth loves the idea, but I think he's pursuing more of a Developer agenda. And Jane Cook, head of facilities management is going to be important in getting this idea off the ground. Kelly Fitzpatrick, VP of Marketing, will also be instrumental in this. Of course, our CEO, Jesse Babcock, will need to play a prominent role. So will Dr. Warren Shaw, chief of staff at the hospital. And speaking of staff, I'll need to talk with Thomas Johansen, head of all hospital attendants, and Erica Long, head nurse. We'll also need the union rep, Frieda Ruiz, on board. And Larry DeCicco, head of sanitation. Let's see . . . who else? Oh, yeah, Jeff Weaver, our CFO. And I may want to talk with Monroe Moore, the strategy consultant who's been advising Babcock for the past few months. Then, there's Judy Turner, our community relations director. She'll absolutely need to play a role in this. And I guess I'll need to reach out to Broome County's supervisor, Bryan North . . ."

George was well on his way to creating his list of stakeholders.

Step 3: Identify Each Stakeholder's Agenda

With list in hand, now it's time to map the agendas of the stakeholders. You need to go down the list and identify each stakeholder's agenda: Traditionalist, Adjuster, Developer, or Revolutionary.

The best way to identify the agenda of the stakeholder is to remember previous initiatives and recall how they acted at that time. Role-play—get into the shoes of the other person. Try to anticipate the behavior of the other. Ask yourself how this particular individual in this particular division will react to this particular idea. How will this reaction trigger a reaction in others in the organization? Recall a person's specific attitude and behavior from the past and try to extrapolate into the future. These historical scenarios will allow you to anticipate a particular agenda and probable action in the future. If you tell your spouse that you want to invite two or three colleagues to dinner, you say to yourself, "I know how she is going to react." Just as you may know what your wife may think about having coworkers over to dinner, you can also anticipate the reaction of your colleagues as you suggest to them that you should centralize all the clerical operation under one director.

One would hope that you've had more experience in anticipating your spouse than your work colleagues, but in truth, it may be easier to anticipate the agendas of workplace colleagues than to anticipate the agenda of a spouse. In the workplace, issues are limited. The depth of knowledge and the detail of historical experiences are fairly incomplete. Also, in the workplace, you can try to map through discovery, if not gossip. Ask others their views on how a particular person will react to an idea or has generally reacted in the past. The trick here, of course, is to do this in a manner that doesn't telegraph your intentions. Subtlety is vital. You need not be scientific about mapping the agendas of others. Your list will always be subject to inaccuracies. But if you're 80 percent correct, you'll be well armed for your battles, for your conversations, and for your other support-building activities.

∾

Now that George Irwin had developed his list of stakeholders, he thought about each of them. Jane Cook, the head of facilities management at the hospital, thought the idea had merit, but didn't think the organization should move too quickly on George's idea. Jane was concerned that the organization didn't have the capacity to expand the number of facilities they managed. Deep down inside, Jane was perfectly comfortable with her span of control and had finally stabilized the operations in her organization. A large-scale facilities expansion might be good for her, but she was also concerned that the initiative might disrupt the current chain of command and she'd end up reporting to a new head of facilities management. Jane has a Developer agenda. She seems inclined to support George, but there are issues that keep her from being an outright ally.

Thomas Johansen had other ideas. Thomas is a managing director, responsible for all hospital attendants. When George shared with Thomas his vision of the satellites, Thomas dismissed the idea as unimaginative and with the potential to bring down the reputation of the hospital. Though George didn't dig much further, Thomas's real concern was that the need for hospital attendants would be minimal in satellites, thereby diluting his relative power in the organization. Thomas also had some suspicions that one of his direct reports—an ambitious, young MBA—was trying to carve out his own position in the organization and he felt threatened. As a result, Thomas didn't see the need for change and would do what he could to stop such efforts. Thomas is clearly pursuing a Traditionalist agenda.

Broome County Sisterhood also had Adjusters. Kelly Fitzpatrick, VP of marketing, was a fairly prominent one. George recalled her reaction at a recent meeting when he innocently suggested an idea he had for an Internet marketing initiative. She lambasted him for moving in on her turf without consulting her. George visualized this meeting with Kelly and decided it was better to get her input on the idea rather than to try to sell her on it. Kelly heard of George's idea, sat back in her chair, stared out the window, then turned to him and said: "George, I hear what you're saying and I agree—we could be doing a much better job of getting closer to our customers. I've been lobbying hard for a new Customer Relationship Management system for my organization and I think that by adopting that, we may be much better positioned to identify and serve our hard-to-reach customers without making major investments in real estate, parking lots, and buildings. While I appreciate your idea, we're just not anywhere near ready to undertake something of that magnitude. And we haven't proven it would even work!" George left the meeting slightly deflated. That's often what happens when a Revolutionary agenda encounters an Adjuster agenda.

George continued working on his list.

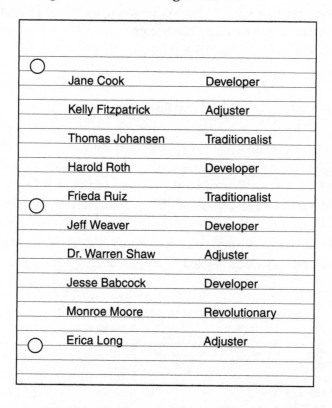

○	Jane Cook	Developer
	Kelly Fitzpatrick	Adjuster
	Thomas Johansen	Traditionalist
	Harold Roth	Developer
○	Frieda Ruiz	Traditionalist
	Jeff Weaver	Developer
	Dr. Warren Shaw	Adjuster
	Jesse Babcock	Developer
	Monroe Moore	Revolutionary
○	Erica Long	Adjuster

As George developed his list, his exuberance was tempered. He noted that there was only one other stakeholder with a Revolutionary agenda—and that guy was a consultant! He has what he thinks is a great idea. But now he recognizes that there are several key people in the organization who may be less than enthusiastic about his idea.

George thought, "How can I move the mindsets of my skeptics—like Jane Cook, Thomas Johansen, and Kelly Fitzpatrick—in such a way that they can become more 'Revolutionary' and supportive of my initiative than they are today?"

Step 4: Analyze Your Allies and Resistors

The following matrix will help you determine where the likely sources of resistance will surface (e.g., does it have to do with particular issues or is it more pervasive?). In this matrix your change agenda goes down the first column and your stakeholders' change agenda goes along the top row. So, find your agenda and go across until you find their agenda. You'll see a box that identifies how well aligned your approaches to change are.

Stakeholder's Agenda

		Traditionalist	Adjuster	Developer	Revolutionary
Your Agenda	Traditionalist	Allies	Potential Allies	Potential Resistors	Resistors
	Adjuster	Potential Allies	Allies	Resistors	Potential Resistors
	Developer	Potential Resistors	Resistors	Allies	Potential Allies
	Revolutionary	Resistors	Potential Resistors	Potential Allies	Allies

There are four potential responses. First is the Allies response. This is the situation where you and your stakeholders generally share the same idea about how change should happen. The second response is Potential Allies. In this situation, you may agree on the change goal, but you disagree on the approach by which change should be implemented. The third response is Potential Resistors. You and the stakeholder don't share goals for change, but you have a common management approach. The fourth response is Resistors. Resistors are at the opposite end of the change spectrum from you—both in terms of goals and management approach.

With your constituency mapped out, it's time to look for patterns, groupings, and overall assessments. Follow these steps:

1. *Highlight all the people who share your agenda.* If you've chosen a Developer agenda, highlight all others pursuing a Developer agenda. These are likely to be your closest allies. They are, fundamentally, in harmony with your perspective on the extent of change needed and how change should be implemented. It will take more than just knowing they *may* be in your camp, you are going to need to cultivate your relationship with them and keep them strongly supportive of your initiative.

2. *Highlight those whose agenda is your exact opposite.* On the matrix, that is the agenda diagonally opposite yours. This is the group you may never be able to change or

influence directly. They will likely be some of your strongest skeptics, so you'll need to develop strategies to keep them from derailing your efforts.

3. *Highlight those who share your goals.* This group will likely support where you are going, but they may disagree with your means for getting there. While they may be potential allies, they are equally likely to be strong adversaries.

4. *Highlight those who share similar approaches to achieving goals, but may not share your defined goals.* This group could be supportive of your efforts, but due to your competing goals, it is more likely that they will be resistors.

George went back to his list. "Okay, I got Monroe Moore as my only other Revolutionary. So, I need to set up a meeting with him and get him on board. If I can do that, that'd go a long way with Babcock. He's one of the managers pursuing a Developer agenda—along with Jane, Bryan, Jeff, and Harold. They seem to like my idea but think my approach is too risky. So, I'm going to need to understand how they'd propose we move ahead. The good news is they like my idea. And I can be flexible in how we get there . . . as long as it's quick!

"Thomas Johansen, Frieda Ruiz, and Larry DeCicco are going to be trouble," George thought. "Moving them will be like trying to pick up the entire hospital and move it down the street. I've got to figure out how to keep them from undermining me. They really are the key to the success of this thing and all of them have a lot of influence with Babcock and with Harold Roth.

"Then there are Kelly Fitzpatrick, Dr. Shaw, and Erica Long. They're going to be tough nuts. They don't seem to want to change much. When they do choose to change, they really take action and push things ahead—my kind of approach. But they seem only to see the downside to my idea."

Allies and Resistors

You will need different strategies for dealing with the four different groups that arise in response to your idea. The easiest to deal with, naturally, are the Allies, the people who think, "This is it!" when they hear your idea. They are sold from the beginning. You have a common agenda; they share your goal and the approach by which you want to implement the change. With Allies, you've got three challenges: You want to solidify them, coalesce them, and get them behind you in a solid and consolidated way.

Second, you have the Potential Allies, those who are sitting on your side of the fence. You share similar goals, but your management approach is different. You want them to jump off the fence into your yard. Potential Resistors are also on the fence, but with their legs dangling on the other side. They are likely to share your management approach, but disagree with you on goals. You want to neutralize their influence or you want them to move closer to your side of the fence.

Resistors are just that. They disagree with you on goals and their management approach is the opposite of yours. Like the Potential Resistors, you do what you can to neutralize them, but you wouldn't mind if they spent more time closer to your fence.

How do you distribute your effort in getting support from the four camps of allies and resistors? If you see that your allies are willing to support you, but are not behind you 100 percent, the first thing you need to do is coalesce your base. You have to make sure that your allies are with you solidly. Get them to rally around your idea. Your next step is to move your potential allies along to get them on your side of the fence. You want to begin to persuade them, to argue why they should join your effort. Third, you'll then be able to approach your potential resistors and resistors and say, "Look! We already have strong support from others in the organization. Won't you consider coming along?" You have to deal with all three of these groups.

Don't wait to deal with potential resistors and resistors. If you wait too long, what will happen is that potential resistors will become bona fide resistors who will slip away beyond your grasp. They'll resist even more strongly and become even more entrenched in their position. They'll have a sense, perhaps with reason, that they are only an afterthought. If you deal with the resistors too early, on the other hand, you'll come to them from a weak position. The trick is to deal with the resistors when they know that you already have a groundswell of support, but that the game isn't over and that there is still room for negotiation. In the next part of the book, you'll learn how to get all of these groups on your side.

Part II

Get Them on Your Side

Chapter 5

Create Your Coalition

The initiative about which you are so passionate has by now generated a fair amount of resistance. Some of it comes from obvious places, while other detractors have caught you by surprise. You've identified some of your resistors and potential allies as having tinkering goals while others have overhauling goals. You know which have improvising and which have planning management approaches. Most important, you've begun to understand their agendas. Some are Traditionalists or Adjusters, and others Developers or Revolutionaries. Now your challenge is to get them to coalesce around your effort.

Today, there are few lone heroes, and even fewer positions that command enough power to get results without allies. Instead, you need to pursue a model of change that politicians, labor leaders, and public policy advocates have been using effectively for years: the art and science of building coalitions.

Without a coalition, you are a lone wolf in the organization—where the risk is much greater than any likely reward. With a coalition, you improve the chances of implementing your proposal successfully, of surviving unintended consequences of your initiative, and of enhancing your position for pursuing future opportunities. In this sense, the ability to build coalitions in organizations today is not just a skill—it is a necessity for survival and success. More often than not, through mobilizing groups of people and resources, you can attain the influence and power to take action and bring about change.

A coalition has a protective and a harmonizing function. By having others join you, you are less vulnerable and more protected. Moreover, you can harmonize your differences and reduce resistance, pursuing at least the appearance of a common course of action.

Formally defined, a coalition is a politically mobilized collection of interest groups or individuals committed to achieving a common outcome (i.e., resistance or change).* Through political mobilization you create a group that has some sense of shared goals and/or a sense of connected interests. A coalition is an alliance for joint action.

---

* In political science the classic work in coalitions remains William H. Riker's *The Theory of Political Coalitions* (Yale University Press, 1962). While this theme has yet to become a major thrust, some of the classic works dealing with it include Cyert and March's *A Behavioral Theory of the Firm* (Prentice-Hall, 1963) and James D. Thompson's *Organizations in Action* (McGraw Hill, 1967). In the specific context of change, see Rosabeth Moss Kanter's *The Change Masters* (Touchstone, 1983).

How big does this alliance have to be to be considered a coalition? Well, when your husband and son are trying to convince you that it is a good idea to take two days to go to Tucson to get away from the miserable, dirty snow of Manhattan; when your son laments that he needs a break but that he could take his homework with him; when your husband reinforces it, telling you that you have plenty of frequent flyer miles—they are acting as a coalition. A coalition can even be two against one.

But a coalition cannot be just any two people. It has to consist of two people who somehow share common agendas, goals, and means. A coalition is comprised of people who have a common approach, or at a minimum, people who can negotiate mutually acceptable agendas, goals, means, and approaches.

You may like the guy in marketing, but the two of you may have no overlapping agenda, no overarching need. The only thing you have in common is the elevator. That is not a coalition. Here are some hallmarks of true coalitions:

1. A coalition is a conscious relationship with the intention of trying to get something done. Within your marketing division, the two associates in charge of northern New Jersey come to you and tell you that they think the time has come to expand the territory into western Pennsylvania to include the city of Scranton. When they approach you with each reinforcing the other's idea, they are acting as a coalition.

2. A coalition is made up of people who want to influence, want to take action, and want to cause some sort

of change by acting together. In that sense, often coalitions are made up of people with no real authority in the organization, but who seek to have an impact on the direction the organization—the department, the unit—is moving.

3. A successful coalition must find the balance between the self-interested goals of the individual members and the collective goal of the group itself. When trying to coalesce individuals around your agenda, the test of your political competence is your ability to change the focus of the key actors from their individual self-interest to the interest of the collective.

When you shift into a coalition state of mind, you begin to see that the action you are seeking is the beginning of a multi-step campaign whose success is based on the assumption that you can get others to join you. In that sense, coalitions are a proactive mode of enhancing participation.

It is almost an accepted truism these days that organizations want to nurture participation. The more participation you have, the greater the input you will get, and the greater the diversity of knowledge, the higher the reliability of the emergent ideas and the greater the probability of success.

What does participation mean? Does it simply mean getting input? I am reminded of a late-night discussion I once participated in during the 1980s at a convention of school superintendents. A superintendent from a neighboring state ranted and raved about how he was committed to participation. How input was a critical factor. How suggestion boards posted throughout the schools increased teachers' contributions to his decisions. How he attended committee meetings and gave each teacher time to speak his or her mind. At one point he opened his coat and revealed a walkie-talkie. "This allows me to stay in touch." (This was before cell phones.) Is that participation? Is participation something we give to others?

When people speak of participation, they often speak as if it is something that is theirs to give: "I give you the power to participate." Beneath this veneer of egalitarianism is the very undemocratic notion that the right of participation is something that managers give workers. There is a paternalistic quality about it—more like "I give my son the right to speak," rather than accepting his inherent right to speak. This is reflected in the current trend toward empowerment.

Talk to any politically correct manager and mention that they need to engage in the politics of negotiating coalitions and their reaction is that there is something repugnant about it. "But we meet all the time," said one manager friend of mine. "I am perpetually engaged in dialogue. I give them the forum to say whatever they want. On top of that, I don't like being political. A coalition is so political." Not really. Participation and empowerment is an elitist management model. A coalition campaign is a democratizing force in organizations.

When you campaign to establish a coalition, the message you're sending to your potential allies is that they are important, they are powerful, and you need their support. You need them to join you. Establishing a coalition is distinctly different from "giving" through participation or empowerment. Coalitions are based on your recognition of others as critical to the political reality of getting something done.

Think of coalitions as enablers. Coalitions enable you to keep your initiative alive and achieve your goals. While coalitions of some type are needed for virtually any implementation effort, they are integral to and a requirement for success when any or all of the following three conditions exist:

1. Your initiative has far-reaching consequences.
2. Your efforts have a perceived high risk and complexity.
3. Your initiative vies for scarce resources.

Dealing with Far-Reaching Consequences

When trying to take action that has far-reaching consequences, the politically competent leader realizes that he or she must have a coalition of support. In dealing with an issue with far-reaching consequences, political leaders must make sure that before they push too far ahead that they've established a coalition, a sense of a mandate.

Far-reaching consequences are natural by-products of initiatives that challenge the routine, the traditional, the expected mode of behavior. Far-reaching consequences are often referred to as *paradigm shifts*, those actions that make us look at something from a different perspective or pursue an unexpected goal. If mishandled, and not supported by a coalition, these challenging and often creative initiatives could have potentially destructive consequences.

When Israeli Prime Minister Yitzhak Rabin began a dialogue with the PLO in 1993, he understood that he needed to have the support of a coalition; otherwise this radical proposition had little or no chance of success. Rabin's strength was his political competence—he knew that because of his paradigm-shattering ideas he would need a diversified coalition behind him.

Several years later, Rabin's successor, Ehud Barak, was criticized for attending the Mideast peace summit at Camp David with Yasser Arafat and President Bill Clinton without a mandate—that is, without a coalition. His failure of leadership was a failure in political competence. He didn't understand that he had to do his political homework before pushing a far-reaching idea. He failed to recognize the need for a coalition.

When Lou Gerstner decided to move IBM from a computer products company to a technology service company, providing what he called "solutions for a small planet," the shift had dramatic implications at all levels of the organization (e.g., sales, human resources, marketing, finance).

In these instances, no matter who proposed the change—Rabin, Barak, or Gerstner—the proposed change was inconsistent with the norms of their respective organizations, and, as such, it was critical for them to create tentative support from a coalition.

అ

For another example of the need for coalition building, consider a prestigious university's investment in online learning. After several years of watching other top universities invest heavily in online education, Bill Declan, a senior officer at one university, believed he had a better model. Declan developed a model that integrated online learning with traditional classroom learning and was seeking several million dollars in seed funding to get the initiative off the ground. For a 150-year-old institution, this proposal was nothing short of revolutionary, and it was no surprise that the effort was hotly contested.

Think about the far-reaching implications that this venture represented. From the academic perspective, the pedagogy of this online model was untested and its quality was not at all assured. And if it succeeded, it would fundamentally change the way education was delivered at the university.

From a financial perspective, this model would change the university's fundamental business model—adding new levels of financial risk and volatility of returns. From an operations standpoint, the logistics of running a world-class online education program were still unknown. The venture required people, knowledge, and skills that the university had not traditionally employed.

From a student-recruitment perspective, a shift toward online learning would now require much more proactive marketing and even direct sales efforts—something that only existed in remote areas of the university's traditional activities. And from

an alumni-relations perspective, the impact that online education would have on feelings of affiliation to one's school—and
on alumni contributions to the university—was virgin territory.

At one level, this online education initiative was a fairly
simple set of experiments in learning. At another level, this initiative had the potential to uproot virtually every department
within the university. And it was not at all clear that it would
be for the better.

For Bill to be successful with an initiative with such far-
reaching and unknowable implications, he had to find a broad
base of support. If he charged ahead without building support
in the finance department of the school, or without bringing
along a handful of senior faculty members, or without engaging
the development office, it would be highly unlikely that his initiative would have a chance of survival. Even if Bill were able
to make some progress without any support, the first sign of
failure—such as poor initial enrollment—could bring down the
initiative—not to mention Bill's career at the university.

Like Bill, if you decide to change your organization's goals,
culture, structure, or work process in a way that has little or
no precedent, it is critical that you form a coalition. If there is
no precedent, no historical context for the particular change
you have in mind, you better have others around you who
will legitimize your effort. Getting people on your side and
mobilizing your coalition is critical when your idea is far-
reaching, out of the ordinary, out of the norm, or when your
idea does not follow the standard operating procedure of the
organization.

Dealing with Risk and Complexity

When your effort has a high level of perceived risk and complexity, you will face much more resistance and opposition
than you would for low-risk or less complex projects. The more
complex the effort, the more you'll need allies with whom to
exchange knowledge, discuss tactics, and deflect criticism. It's
easy to underestimate potential resistance as well as the complexity of your initiative, and thus, you may be unaware of how
critical the formation of a coalition may be to your success.

꙳

Jason was a marketing manager at an Indianapolis-based
consumer products firm that specialized in certified organic
products. Jason had decided, after careful analysis, to begin
offering a 5 percent discount on all breakfast cereals sold to large
supermarkets and price clubs. Based on his assessment, the discount would boost sales by 15 percent or more and help the firm
better compete in the lucrative cereal business. Jason informed
his boss, Latisha, of his plan. She thought it sounded great, but
she asked him to check with Karl, the unit's sales manager.

When Jason told Karl about the discount, Karl looked at
Jason as if he'd told him his bonus check had gotten lost in the
mail. "Are you crazy? Do you have any idea what a pain in the
#$?*@/ that would be? First of all, I'd have to get our national
sales team together to plan and announce the program. Then,
we'd need to develop collateral material to support our effort.

Then, we'd need to make changes to our bonus compensation system to accommodate the discounts. Jason, you probably didn't think you'd ever hear a salesperson telling you they didn't want the opportunity to lower prices, but this may create more problems than any of my salespeople would find financially beneficial."

Jason mentioned his plan to the breakfast cereal production manager, Sari, who also had some concerns. "Jason, we are right about at our production capacity for breakfast cereals. If we add a significant increase to our production requirements, we're going to have to look for an additional factory. That may end up costing us some money. It may be significant."

Jason also spoke with his buddy, Ray, in the IT department. Ray scratched his head for a minute and then said, "Don't tell anyone this, but our invoices don't accommodate a field for that kind of discount. It'd require a whole new system or some pretty major programming to pull it off. But I think we need to face this issue head-on. If you move ahead with it, I'll make the programming happen. But we'll need to do an end run on this one. There's no way I'd get this project through the budget cuts in my department. Let's just do it, Jas."

Finally, Karen, the product manager for the company's hot cereals, came up to Jason and said, "Hey, rumor has it you're going to cut prices by 5 percent. Let me just tell you that if you go that route, you're going to put my business in the sewer. Every retailer will expect my prices to drop, too. And with the margins we work with, there's no way I could remain viable.

Listen, just back off that idea—we're already facing pricing confusion with you guys as it is. Don't make it worse."

As you can see, Jason's simple idea of a 5 percent discount isn't at all a simple idea. It is also an idea that has a fair amount of risk and potential expense associated with it. If Jason tries to take this initiative on alone, he'll be toast before he even gets out of his office. The only way Jason can succeed with a complex and potentially risky initiative like this is to build himself a coalition of support.

While the need for change in Indianapolis seems simple to Jason, the change agenda revealed itself to be complex and risky. Jason thought change would be as basic as a small discount in the product. Other actors perceived the situation differently from the change agent.

What Jason failed to recognize was that unilateral action, by its very nature, creates opposition. To control change and diffuse opposition, you need to form a coalition. Mobilizing your coalition is critical when your proposal is complex or when others see the perceived risk of implementation of the idea as great.

Competing for Scarce Resources

As the environment becomes leaner, should you form a coalition? Should you put all your emphasis on one particular change effort even if you are fully aware that this means that you will take away resources from other change efforts? What you need to do is to coalesce.

You have the idea to redesign your marketing division. You've decided to restructure the division top to bottom. This redesign effort will mean that you will have to ignore other divisions at the same time and that you will not be able to put resources into other change efforts. It is paramount for you to mobilize other workers, managers, and supervisors around your effort. If you don't, they are likely to see your efforts as taking away from their interests, they may perpetually snipe at your attempts, and inevitably, sabotage any success you bring about. However, if you mobilize a coalition around a common agenda, you will be able to delay and diffuse these difficulties.

ℒ

Donna, a human resources manager at a state environmental protection agency, was working on her budget for the upcoming fiscal year. She had a lot on her plate. The agency was greatly expanding its water safety initiative and would need to make a big hiring push for program administrators and customer service representatives. Donna was evaluating a new HRIS (Human Resource Information System) for the agency and really wanted to implement it in the coming year. She also was in the process of developing a state-of-the-art training program on deforestation, which was mandated training for anyone who worked in one of the 279 state parks. And, lastly, Donna wanted to bring in a large HR consulting firm to advise her on the latest proposal to reorganize the agency by district, rather than by environmental problem area.

Donna's problem was that she could not do all of these things with her unit's tight budget. But her dilemma wasn't as simple as choosing two out of the five programs that needed to get done. If she chose not to focus on hiring program administrators and customer service reps, the major water safety effort might be stalled because of Donna's inability to staff it quickly enough. And if she puts off the HRIS system, could the organization really track its growing size and complexity for federal reporting purposes? And if she cuts the training, would a large number of park rangers lose their licenses? Finally, if she passes on the HR consulting firm engagement, would her group be left out of the highly visible reorganization initiative? Or, worse, would senior management's effort become undermined by unanticipated problems that the consultants could have helped them avoid?

If Donna's going to make a decision based on scarce resources, she'd better have people behind that decision—people who might otherwise be vested in one of her initiatives that may not get funded in the coming year.

⁂

Getting people on your side through mobilization is critical when resources are scarce. Coalitions are vital when your initiative faces far-reaching consequences, perceived high risk and complexity, or scarce resources. In each of these instances, coalitions aren't simply nice-to-have or good-corporate-citizen efforts. They are required in order for you to survive, and they are essential to the success of your initiative.

The Importance of Forming Coalitions at Each Stage

Change is a multistep process. Usually, change is thought of as moving from early stages, where the idea is planned, to later stages, where the change effort is put in place and stabilized. Given the ongoing nature of the change process, you'll find that at each stage your objectives and strategies need to be somewhat different. Below is a chart that summarizes the four stages of the change cycle and the importance of forming coalitions at each stage:

Preparing for Change	Initiating Change	Putting Change in Place	Stabilizing Change
Spread risk	Overcome resistance	Avoid sabotage	Deflect revenge
Preempt derailment efforts	Secure legitimacy	Get "over the hump"	Maintain support for next project
Create critical mass			

Preparing for Change

Spread risk: During the earliest stage of your initiative, the risk of failure is at its greatest. Before initiating any change, you should be aware of the risks imposed by the proposed change. You need to think of the downside of the change. In uncertain environments, you need to anticipate and hedge the risks of the change. Hedging risk involves sharing it with others—people within your organization or outside it—who will be engaged in or affected by the change process. When more people in the organization get behind an initiative, each point of support absorbs some of the overall risk of the change effort.

Preempt derailment efforts: Frequently, leaders of change efforts wait until the project is well underway before gathering support. This approach is reactive, rather than proactive. You know your initiative will face resistance. You need to anticipate resistance in order to cope with it.

In the earliest stages of your initiative, unanswered resistance can derail it quickly. From the moment some of your colleagues hear about your effort, they will immediately oppose it. It is impossible to overstate the importance of building a coalition in order to prevent the immediate abortion of your project.

By building a coalition early, you can preempt inevitable resistance. You will never be able to eradicate resistance completely, but having a strong camp of support reduces the risk of opposition and allows you to introduce your idea to a receptive audience.

Create critical mass: Building coalitions early is necessary not only to spread risk and preempt derailment efforts, but also to create critical mass for your initiative. Once your initiative gains critical mass a certain amount of momentum kicks in—making the initiative difficult to stop without coordinated resistance.

After proposing a change effort, it's a race to create critical mass before the resistance mounts. You need to start as early as possible—even before the formal proposal is announced—to seed support for your initiative. The longer it takes to create critical mass, the less likely that your effort will ever achieve it.

Think about how an idea evolves in an organization. Let's say someone at a consumer products company has an idea for a new razor. What happens to that idea early on? It gets discussed. At the outset, the person with the idea shares it with others. If their reaction is positive, the idea will be shared more broadly. For example, "What do you think of a razor with three blades instead of two? I'll be sure to get the closest shave yet." "You may be onto something. Has it been prototyped?" Or, "I don't get it. Why would anyone need a third way to get cut? Will consumers get it?" If the reaction is not positive, the concept may die or it may be shared with a different group of people. During the initial phase of the change process, resistance may surface. In the case of the new razor, resistance may come from the person in charge of the incumbent twin-bladed razor or from someone in the production department. At this early stage, the person with the idea needs to prepare for resistance and build a case to keep any major opposition in check.

The viability of the three-bladed razor is most threatened in this initial period of development.

Initiating Change

Overcome resistance: Resistance to your initiative begins early and can continue throughout the effort. As you attempt to move your proposal forward and negotiate with others who have different agendas, you will need a strong coalition to help you overcome ongoing resistance.

Your opposition may begin with the first meeting, when an authority figure fires across the bow to ascertain how serious you are about an idea. Your opposition may continue to attempt to discredit you and your agenda. It is generally easier to attack an idea than to propose an alternative. However, if the opposition is well organized, they may be able to produce a viable alternative to your effort, with the intention of disrupting or terminating the progress of your initiative.

You need to build your coalition and develop your support to the point where it can overcome whatever resistance may arise. In the early stages, your coalition may not be as strong as you'd like, so you will need to stay focused on strengthening and expanding your camps of support.

Secure legitimacy: In these early stages, your coalition will begin to develop momentum. Coalition members will become more closely tied to your effort and are more likely to actively oppose your resistors. As your initiative builds critical mass, you must continue to strengthen and expand your coalition, as your resistors are not likely to have given up. The support of your idea by others and their willingness to join your coalition legitimizes your agenda and offers support to your logic or arguments for the need for change.

Going back to the razor example, consider what may happen at this stage. The person with the idea for the three-bladed razor has a number of allies, such as the head of the razor division and perhaps the head of sales for the razor division. The union may be behind it, if they see the product as a means of creating or securing new jobs. The originator of the new idea may be able to make a compelling financial case for the new product. By getting a diverse group of allies on board early, the developer of the razor idea builds legitimacy within the organization and creates momentum, enabling him to pre-empt certain types of resistance.

Putting Change in Place

Avoid sabotage: Some of your detractors may become sore losers, and they won't give up easily. Your effort will continue to run the risk of opposition and resistance even after you've started putting change in place. In the later stages, this can take the form of sabotage—where your detractors make both overt and covert attempts to derail your project. If you've continued to nurture and grow your coalition, you may be able to avoid sabotage. Again, by strengthening and expanding your change coalition you not only curb the risk of personal attacks, but also you reduce the risk that your resistors will take further action against you.

Get over the hump: Your objective at this stage is to get your initiative "over the hump." Throughout the process you've been encountering two risks: (1) that your change effort will be overthrown by resistance, and (2) that your change effort won't survive on its own merits. At this stage, the threat both risks pose has been lowered substantially.

This is your last chance for an all-out push in your coalition-building efforts. Target groups that may not have been strategically important early on, but that might now play a more influential role at the later stages of the change cycle. This is when you also need to begin to shift your sight toward your next effort and toward future allies.

By getting the marketing and sales organization behind the three-bladed razor idea, our protagonist at the consumer products company built a very strong and influential coalition. Though resistance may not evaporate entirely, it would be very hard for a resistance movement to derail the effort. There may be further questions about the financial projections and other details of the initiative, but the idea is solidly supported and the focus is more on the new product launch than on whether there will be a new product to launch.

At this point, the initiator of the three-bladed razor is "over the hump." The pressure is—by no means—off. The pressure has shifted from a pressure to survive to a pressure to perform.

Stabilizing Change

Deflect revenge: As your initiative becomes institutionalized, your skeptics still carry on. Any unintended problems that crop up will call your ability and competence into question. Even if you are successful, there will be those who won't hesitate to call you a failure. Your best defense against these shots is a strong coalition—the people and groups who will stifle critics' claims. This is why, even at this late phase, you need to continue nurturing and strengthening the support you've developed along the way. Like minimizing the risk of sabotage efforts, building strong coalitions will make it risky for your resistors to seek revenge.

Maintain support for future projects: After your initiative is in place, you will likely spend more of your time considering your next effort. Your coalition, assuming they were satisfied with the outcome of your recent effort, will be your likeliest source of future backing. Remember, it is rarely too early to begin to build support for your next project.

At this point in our consumer products company example, the three-bladed razor rolls out and is successful. While most in the organization win by this success, clearly, there are some who aren't as well positioned as they were before the idea emerged.

If the three-bladed razor idea was yours or you're one of the key people who moved the idea through to launch, you may have made some enemies. During this stage, you want to focus on continuing to build allies in the organization and to ensure that your detractors do not seek revenge for their losses.

Let's face it: Organizations aren't collections of friends and family who love each other through thick and thin. They are arenas of competition, disagreement, and resistance. As such, there are always people who are trying to move ahead, even at the expense of others. Our change leader at the consumer products company will learn this when the next new idea for a razor emerges. He'll want to make sure that he's fostered productive relationships, even with those who opposed him and lost.

Any effort to make things happen in an organization will likely proceed through these four phases of change. The change cycle can unfold over a matter of weeks or the cycle can take years, depending on the goal and approach of the coalition. While you will never get an e-mail alert saying, "Congratulations, you have completed the Preparing for Change phase" or "Welcome to the Initiating Change phase of your project," you need to constantly be sensitive to where you are in the process—what you need to be doing now and what you need to begin doing soon. If you can keep your sense of where your effort stands, you'll be much better prepared for ensuring its success—and yours.

Chapter 6

Establish Your Credibility

Romi Cruz stared incredulously at his budget for the following year. The bubble had burst on the new economy and the fallout was now pinching museums, which benefited from the stock market run. The Deacon County Museum of Contemporary Art rode on the coattails of the individuals and companies that had succeeded so spectacularly over the past few years.

Annual donations had nearly doubled. Several magnanimous benefactors personally funded the building and curating of brand-new wings of the museum. The museum itself took advantage of its fiscal success by expanding its educational programs and by acquiring a contemporary sculpture collection. Jonathan Edwards, the museum's curator, was able to hire curatorial staff for the photography and sculpture collections. Romi's predecessor, Jackson Tate, had taken advantage of the flood of resources to beef up the membership and education staff. The museum had grown well beyond its grassroots beginnings.

As the once-robust economy stalled, the museum found itself too big for its budget. When Jackson Tate jumped to the directorship of the Old Dominion Museum of Contemporary Art, Romi came on board as his replacement. It was clear to Cruz that the museum—and its staff—needed to recalibrate its activities to reflect the tight economy. They needed to shift their activities from those fueled by growing contributions to the more traditional museum environment of tight budgets and limited resources. Romi had to move the museum staff from their previous goals of innovation and growth to one of conservation—focusing its core collection and reallocating financial resources.

Romi was in the difficult position of having to move the museum staff away from the communal culture that served them well during its early years to a more atomistic one, with discipline as a priority. He knew that his role was to formalize an organization structure that would allow for more controlled decision-making. He needed to remind his staff—and, in some cases, redefine—what each of their responsibilities were and what tasks they needed to carry out. He simply needed to develop a tighter organization.

❧

Romi knew that he faced an uphill battle. The museum staff had gotten used to operating with a high degree of autonomy. When he first started at the museum, Romi encouraged a creative, independent culture. He was going to need to adjust that approach to foster a new environment, and he realized that his success was going to depend on his ability to persuade others to join him in this change effort. Romi needed to mobilize as many museum staff as possible to join his coalition. To do that, he needed to establish his credibility, justify his ideas, get buy-in, and persuade and lead a change coalition.

In establishing his coalition, Romi first needed to achieve a level of credibility. After all, he was new to the museum. Keep in mind that having credibility does not automatically mean that people will accept your ideas. What credibility represents is that others will have trust in your intent and that they will validate or bear witness to the authenticity of your effort. Credibility is dependent on both the worthiness of the idea and your trustworthiness. As such, it is sometimes impossible for others to separate you from your idea. Much depends on whether others view you as having the credibility to push a particular idea forward. Without the perception of others that you have the credibility to push an idea, it is unlikely that you can form, let alone sustain, a coalition.

Your credibility has to do with whether others believe you have the authority to start and implement the change you propose. Credibility is something that others confer on you, not something that you must solicit from them.* In many ways, credibility is an overall evaluation of your right to make a particular suggestion.

Credibility may not guarantee that others will agree with you, but it provides insurance that your suggestion falls within some realm of reasonableness. Credibility implies trust in the broad parameters of what you say.

Credibility is critical to your political competence. Without it, rest assured that people will not get on your side. Before anyone has a chance to question your ideas, they will question you. Who are you to make this suggestion? Why should you be deemed credible? Where do you get your authority?

There are four sources of personal credibility:

1. Positional authority
2. Personal integrity
3. Expertise and knowledge
4. Time and opportunity

Positional Authority

When proposing an idea, the easiest thing to do is to justify the idea on the basis of your position. When you hold a high or influential position in the organization, others generally

---

* There is a tendency to confuse power and credibility. Powerful people may not be credible. For a power discussion of the same issue, see S. B. Bacharach and E. J. Lawler, *Power and Politics in Organizations,* Jossey-Bass, 1980.

assume you have legitimate power behind your initiatives. You are assumed to have access to all the tools needed to wield influence, and if you don't have direct access to the top, you are able to gain access indirectly.

When your detractors initially resist your initiative, having positional authority is a major advantage. Your position, especially if it is high, gives you the type of credibility that makes it difficult for others to challenge you—but it may not be the best type of credibility.

Is it really good enough for you to suggest an idea for change and hope it is viewed as credible simply because you are high up on the totem pole? Such credibility may be the most difficult to challenge, but is it the most sustainable? Do you really want to rely solely on positional authority when establishing yourself as the leader of a coalition? People may join your coalition because they recognize the power of your position in the organization, but are they joining you because they've bought into your initiative?

Just as you can tell your child to do something because you are the parent, or just as the president of the United States can initiate a foreign policy because of his position, that doesn't mean that credibility is lasting. Having positional authority may be a quick and efficient way to marshal a short-term coalition, but it is a questionable method of forming a long-lasting coalition. You will need to do more than rely on your position of power in the organization to establish the long-term legitimacy that you will need to push your change through.

❧

As the new museum director, Romi was in a position to be directive. Though the Deacon County staff had operated quite independently in the past—with an unusual degree of autonomy for a museum—Romi was a different kind of leader. He wasn't exactly a command-and-control type, but he did have a strong sense of process and formality. In his opinion, a museum like Deacon County needed much stronger direction and discipline. It had grown to be a bigger museum, but the staff members were still operating in some ways as if they were a small group of irreverent schoolchildren.

How could Romi use his position to gain the respect and support that he needed to implement his agenda? At his desk, staring at the stainless steel sculpture that stood in the corner of his office, he considered scenarios.

Romi thought, "I could go right into Jonathan's office and lay down the law. I can tell him 'Jon, your spending on new collections has far outpaced our capacity to support those investments. We need to cut back, and to even consider selling some of those pieces that aren't core to our collection.'" Romi thought it over again: "Sure, *that'll* go over well!" He smirked and considered his alternatives: "They know I'm the director and that, ultimately, they report to me. I've got to figure out a way to use that influence in a way that keeps people motivated to change."

After thinking it through further, Romi decided that he'd put together a short presentation outlining the situation and providing his roadmap for getting there. He'd call a staff meeting with his senior people and see how they react to it. "If there is no unanimous objection," Romi thought, "I'll be able to use my position to get others to take responsibility for certain parts of the implementation."

Notice how Romi plays out different scenarios about how to use the power of his position to build credibility for his agenda. Power dynamics play out on both sides. Consider the situation of Mia Stephens and Arnold Hynes, the two newly hired curators. They grabbed a sandwich together and began talking about Romi:

"He seems like a good guy. A little stiff, but all right," said Mia.

"Yeah, but what kind of changes do you think he's going to make?" asked Arnold. "We're the new kids on the block and he is definitely looking to cut costs. Do you think there's any chance that he'll axe our positions?"

"No way. He's got bigger fish to fry—like that bloated development staff. I just hope he lets me move forward with the Huxtable collection I've been pursuing."

"Yeah, I've had my eye on a few pieces that would fill out my area nicely. This job wouldn't be nearly as much fun if he turns me into an exhibit planner."

Even though these stakeholders might resist Romi's change efforts, they understood that, at the end of the day, "What Romi says, goes." This is the benefit of having positional power in an organization. Your job is to leverage that power to your advantage.

❧

Now let's consider someone who chose a more incendiary approach. Chuck McNabb had been promoted to customer service manager. After three and a half years as one of several customer service supervisors, Chuck felt squeezed between his former boss and the seventy-five customer service representatives he oversaw in the telecommunication company's Tucson office. What made him more excited than the promotion itself was that he was finally going to be in a position where he was the "boss." People were finally going to have to march to his orders, rather than pushing back on anything he tried to do as a supervisor.

Chuck's first memo as customer service manager was to announce that he was restructuring the customer service performance metrics. Chuck wanted to reduce the average call time by one minute. He carefully prepared a memo to all customer service reps. He was careful to phrase the directive in a way that would ensure that the unions didn't feel that this was an attempt to reduce the number of reps in the department. He shared it with a buddy of his in marketing and then he sent it out.

About two weeks later, Chuck reviewed the call reports and noticed that average call time had not only NOT decreased, but it had increased by six seconds. Chuck was furious and puzzled. He called in his new customer service supervisor, Rick Decker, and asked him what was going on. "I'm not sure, Chuck. But that memo you sent out sure pissed a bunch of people off."

"What do you mean?"

"Well, these guys have been measured on customer satisfaction levels for a long time. In fact, their union contract was negotiated based on maintaining a high level of customer satisfaction. Now this memo comes along and . . . well, I guess you were never the most popular guy in the group. Now the staff seems confused and a little distrustful of your intentions." Rick had actually held back here on how people really felt and what they really said about Chuck.

Chuck responded, "Don't they understand that I make the rules around here now? This wasn't a request or something that I hadn't thought about carefully. I've been working in this place for over five years. I know what I'm talking about and I'm the manager now. If anyone has a problem with this, you tell them to come to me."

Rick left Chuck's office understanding what it meant to be stuck in the middle.

Chuck sat in his office—furious and frightened. His first move out of the box in a leadership job and people rejected what he ordered. This wasn't how he had imagined this job. Maybe it was the wording of the memo? Chuck thought a bit more. He walked out of his office to go to lunch thinking, "They'll end up listening. After all, I'm the manager of the entire department."

Personal Integrity

If positional authority isn't sufficient for establishing a coalition, you may have to rely on your personal integrity for credibility. People may follow your initial ideas because they assume that you have organizational or personal integrity. They will assume the idea you are proposing is not simply dictated by your own self-interest, but governed by the interest you have in the organization as a whole. Implicit in the notion of personal integrity is the sense that you are a good corporate citizen. Your personal integrity depends on the history of your behavior in the organization. It is your personal history that allows others to suspend negative judgments, even if they do not agree with your initial position. Your personal qualities can stymie early resistance to your change effort.

∾

Romi's museum staff had every right to be skeptical of him. He wasn't an insider in the sense that he didn't rise through the ranks within the museum. Romi came from the outside—from a classical art museum. He had no track record at Deacon County and few people in the organization were able to find out much about him. "He must be hiding something," was how a couple of museum staffers interpreted the lack of dirt on Romi.

Contrast Romi's mysterious background with Jonathan Edwards's track record. Jonathan embodied the personality and soul of Deacon County Museum. Although he was frequently criticized as being arrogant and standoffish, no one disputed Jonathan's commitment to a high-quality, creative center of contemporary art. No one ever accused Jonathan of not saying exactly what was on his mind. In that sense, Jonathan was transparent and highly respected in the organization. With thirteen years of solid experience at Deacon County Museum, he had all the credibility that any director or curator would ever want.

❧

Because Romi's flawless record of leading financially sound museums—and leading them with the highest levels of integrity—is more hearsay than fact to the museum staff, Romi will have to build his integrity within the context of this organization, which he can only do through action and with experience. Though you may believe yourself to have a high level of integrity, others will be skeptical until proven wrong. In today's environment—where leader after leader is found to have flawed integrity—your job of building credibility through personal integrity becomes even more important.

Having personal integrity does not mean that you are totally altruistic and will sacrifice yourself for the organization, but rather that your personal advancement will only occur in the context of organizational rules and that your goals are aligned with the best interests of the organization. While the change may benefit you in some way, others need to know that if you suggested it, it will also greatly benefit the organization.

If you have a history of personal integrity, you get the equivalent of an advance-to-go-and-collect-$200 card that will carry you over to the next round. You've been able to build up enough credibility and goodwill in the organization to make it difficult for your detractors to be openly critical early on. If you have strong personal integrity, skeptics run the risk of having their own agenda questioned when they take potshots at you.

When forming a coalition, you should candidly consider the history of your own integrity. If you know that your history is questionable, you should try to get people with personal credibility who can enhance your coalition to join you.

Expertise and Knowledge

You may have positional authority. You may even have personal integrity, but, when push comes to shove, your credibility also has to rely on your expertise. Inevitably, you are going to have to communicate that you have the know-how to back up your initial idea. Sure, you may be the person in charge. You may even be someone people trust, but why should they get on your side if they are not sure that you know in detail what you are talking about? You are going to have to let people know that your expertise is relevant to the topic at hand. Position and integrity are not substitutes for expertise.

Expertise is having a specialized type of knowledge, such as scarce technical knowledge, skills, or a distinctive package of experience that is relevant to your proposal. An expert has the ability to see a problem from a uniquely specialized perspective and controls unique knowledge resources not readily available to others. Expertise is having the ability in a particular arena to define a problem and come up with a solution.

In highly uncertain times—and in areas that are impacted by technologies—expertise becomes even more useful and valuable to an organization. Since many experts are difficult to replace, expertise further enhances your power and credibility in the organization.

There are multiple types of expertise within an organization, each appropriate for resolving different problems. Technical expertise may be the knowledge held by a recent graduate from Stanford who knows more about cutting-edge information systems than any organizational veteran. The fact that he has a degree in engineering and has written a paper on the future of chip technology may show that he has a degree of credibility, but that credibility exists only in the realm of technological change.

Political expertise is the knowledge you've gained over the years by being a member of the organization. Your experience has taught you how to push an idea through the system—how to best come up with a solution to an internal administrative problem and how to avoid the invisible political obstacles.

External expertise is the knowledge you have about the outside environment: the economy, politics, and the market. For example, in a marketing division individuals with external expertise are often seen as boundary spanners. They'll scout the environment and gather intelligence on behalf of the organization. They are the ones who try to anticipate customer needs, new competitors, new political crises, etc. This boundary-spanning role often lends them a great deal of credibility in their organization.

Over Romi Cruz's twenty-one-year museum career, he has spent very little time with the curators. Romi's strength has been in managing the financial and marketing side of the museum activities. When it came to decisions regarding specific collections and the importance of a particular work, Romi was out of his area of expertise. His strategic planning skills landed him this new job in the first place. Romi now needed to bring that expertise to bear on an entirely new museum staff.

The remarks of Romi's skeptics echoed in the museum's basement hallways: "What does he know about contemporary art? I don't care how financially savvy he is, pricing in contemporary art is just different." . . . "Yeah, and from what I hear, he's never really been involved in a major new membership drive." . . . "How can a bean counterevaluate the importance of our collection? We better watch out before we end up sacrificing our reputation for some short-term financial gain."

Clearly, Romi had his work cut out for him if he was going to try to make changes to the curatorial and membership activities. He knew it. But he also understood that he had the knowledge and experience in running a high-quality, financially sound, world-class museum. So he needed to focus on that expertise and try to use that credibility to effect the changes he wanted in areas that weren't his strength.

❧

Any expertise adds to your credibility as a change leader. In the best of all worlds, you would draw on all three areas of expertise when you want to get them on your side and win support for your initiative. It would be nice if you could say that you know what the problem is because of your engineering background. It would be wonderful to add that your political experience in the organization will allow you to push the idea through. It would be excellent if you could also maintain that your boundary-spanning activity has sensitized you to the market needs and possible pitfalls of this change. It is, however, unlikely that any one person would have expertise in those three areas. As those with specialized knowledge climb the organizational ladder—and move from technical experts to managers—their technical expertise may become dated. Expertise gained in one area may be rendered ineffective if the "expert" moves into another area of the organization.

In forming an initial coalition, you should attempt to make it obvious that you have the critical expertise necessary for proposing and pushing a particular idea. If you don't have that expertise, you have to quickly show exactly how you intend to get it.

Time and Opportunity

Sometimes being in the right place at the right time will give you access to people, information, and knowledge that would otherwise not be available. In a dynamic working environment, it is possible to stumble onto this kind of credibility.

But credibility from opportunity can disappear as quickly as it comes. Opportunities come and go, but so do the players. As a result, credibility from opportunity may be the least stable. But while you have it, it can be a very powerful force against the camps trying to delegitimize your effort.

Often people with time-and-opportunity credibility may be quite eager to initiate change. Because of their sense of immediacy, they are often the ones most capable of seeing the need for a quick-acting coalition. At the same time, they may be the people least capable of initiating a coalition because they may lack credibility in the other areas.

❧

Romi knew his window of opportunity was small. If he didn't get some quick wins early on, the museum staff would perceive him as ineffective and making any change would become progressively harder. Romi also knew that the economy would eventually turn around soon and he'd lose one of the more compelling cases for change: the tight economy. Romi felt like this was the time to seize the opportunity to get his agenda rolling.

You may be able to create a sense of urgency based on time and opportunity, but at the same time you should expand your credibility by bringing in individuals who have their own credibility based on position, integrity, or expertise.

Consider the case of Citibank during the early 1990s—a period of organizational crisis. (In this account, I am drawing on my discussions with former Citibank vice president James Biolos.) Citibank's business faltered—with huge real estate loan losses and tremendous shortfalls in Mexico and South America. The company teetered on the brink of bankruptcy. During this crisis, the CEO, a chaos theorist, implemented a turnaround strategy that concentrated on having a highly decentralized and loosely structured organization.

The CEO developed a "five-point plan" to bring the global banking giant back to financial and operational stability, and he needed to communicate the essence of that plan—and a focus on progress along that plan—to Citibank's global employees frequently and consistently. The vice president of corporate communications, who previously did not have any explicit power or credibility in the organization, suddenly was in the constant presence of the CEO.

In a matter of months, the VP had moved from being a marginal senior player to one of the key players on the CEO's team. In an organization that once valued highly local information and insider knowledge, the need had now shifted to centralized, public communication. This gave the VP extraordinary latitude and enabled him to implement certain initiatives that he could not have pushed through prior to the company's crisis. Even after Citibank stabilized and embarked on one of its more sustained periods of long-term growth, the VP was well positioned to build his power base and take advantage of being in the right position at the right time.

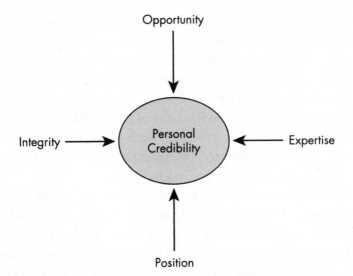

In order to establish personal credibility,* you must use language and personal presentation. How do you let others know, without shoving it down their throat, that you are credible? What language should you use to initiate a supportive response? Keep in mind that if you become overbearing, it is unlikely that you'll develop deep support. If you try to make yourself

---

* This notion of personal credibility is based on Max Weber's discussion of the power basis of legitimacy. In *Economy and Society* (Bedminster Press, 1968), Weber made it clear that the key for any effort to take action—and to have others follow you—was what he referred to as legitimacy. How legitimate do others view the institution? In this book we speak not of legitimacy, but of credibility. Credibility has much more to do with the individual's presentation of self, rather than that of the institution.

credible simply based on your position, you'll be viewed as confusing power with credibility. If you constantly try to push your personal integrity, you may be quickly dismissed as wallowing in self-righteousness and will become an irresistible target for cynics. If you overplay your hand by maintaining that you have the needed expertise, you may be written off as arrogant. Finally, if you claim to be credible because you are at the right place at the right time and have a sense of urgency, you may be viewed as being frantic.

Try to communicate a balanced picture of credibility. Let your colleagues know about your expertise and knowledge, show them your personal integrity, hint about your positional authority, and remind them that you are at the right place at the right time. Most important, don't overplay any single factor and communicate with self-assured subtlety.

Chapter 7

Get Initial Support

Even after you've established your credibility, you are not just going to charge straight ahead with your idea. You are going to have to get initial support. You have to ask yourself who you will invite on board first and how you are going to present the idea to them.

Identifying the people you'll need to get initial support may be critical in sustaining and legitimizing the momentum of your effort. Who are the first few people you want to persuade to join your coalition? Specifically, who are the people you want support from first? Who are the people who offer you the highest level of organizational validation? Who are those who can bear witness to the worthiness of you and your ideas enabling you to get others to give your ideas a hearing?

❧

Janet Rich was a high-flying and relatively young product manager in the consumer products segment of a large pharmaceutical firm. Janet had just finished a meeting with the R&D people and couldn't stop thinking about the calcium-fortified chewing gum that they discussed with her. She thought the product could really take off. The popularity of calcium-enriched products was booming, but Janet felt that there still was a lot of opportunity in the market. Her firm didn't have a strong line of calcium-fortified products or a particularly good chewing gum business. In fact, the chewing gum unit had been on the block for almost a year, and garnered no serious offers.

As highly regarded as she was in the organization, she knew this would be an uphill battle. But there were few strong ideas that Janet could champion and so she felt the need to act soon. After going through all of the potential allies and influential people who might have a stake in this initiative, Janet checked off three names of people she would need initial support from in a way that would help her build support for her effort. First was the category manager for consumer products—her boss's boss. Next was Darryl Wu, one of the firm's chief scientists, who had the ear of several key executives in the organization. The last was the head of large retail accounts for the division. This product would live or die on the shelves of supermarket and drugstore chains, so someone in sales had to get behind it. Janet needed to think about her next steps carefully.

There are three strategies you can use for seeking initial support for your effort: utilizing like minds, co-opting leaders, and incorporating groups.

Utilizing Like Minds

The strategy of utilizing like minds occurs when you identify people whose agendas are more closely aligned with yours and try to persuade them to support your effort. Those with Revolutionary agendas will seek other Revolutionaries; Adjusters will gravitate toward other Adjusters; Developers will pick out other Developers; and Traditionalists will select fellow Traditionalists.

When you seed your coalition by utilizing like minds, you look around and try to carefully choose those individuals whom you feel will share your agenda. This strategy involves having your change effort validated by individuals who think like you, irrespective of whether they are formal leaders. You are most comfortable getting initial support from people who "think like you."

♈

Let's return to the Deacon County Museum of Contemporary Art. Mia Stephens and Arnold Hynes joined the Deacon County Museum as curators just before Romi Cruz was hired. They had been with the museum for only three months before he arrived. Both saw their future success dependent on the ability of the museum to make the transition to a lean museum. In many ways, both were outsiders, but whatever small amount of insider credentials they had could provide Romi with a foothold of support. Romi recognized this immediately. They must feel as he did, he thought, that the museum's culture was a little out of whack with its size. Romi could see in their faces that things didn't work in this organization quite as they had in their previous museum experiences. If Romi could tap into this shared sentiment, he'd have an excellent chance of bringing them on board with his change effort. And even though Mia and Arnold reported directly to Jonathan Edwards, Romi felt that culturally, he and the new curators were closer to each other than they were to their boss.

Mia and Arnold are pursuing classic Developer agendas. They are not Revolutionaries like Romi, but they understand that incremental changes need to be made now if the museum—and their particular area within it—is going to survive in a tighter economy. They might be ideal targets for initial support, ideal early members of Romi's change coalition. If Romi chooses to rely on them in the early stages of forming his coalition, he would need to negotiate with them quietly to solidify their commitment. By keeping the discussions quiet, Romi wouldn't have to deal with too many people, and later, he would be able to build his coalition around Stephens and Hynes. Romi knows that he is dealing with the direct reports of Jonathan Edwards, perhaps the most influential person in the museum's organization. So, this is not a situation where

Romi can just run roughshod through Edwards's organization. He needs discretion, tact, and a good understanding of how Mia and Arnold think about key issues.

✌

The utilization of like minds, coalescing with people who share your agenda, is a coalition formation strategy that often begins with word of mouth. With this approach, potential coalition members will informally spread the word and make known their support to others in the organization, thereby getting more people on your side.

Utilizing like minds is a common strategy for quickly enlisting coalition members and getting some initial support. It requires the least amount of your time and only a low level of involvement from the potential coalition member. The downside to utilizing like minds is that, because you are selecting individuals who share your intentions, you may quickly form a small group that reinforces a common belief. You may unwittingly form a group that others in the organization may view as a cult. When utilizing like minds, you can often find yourself preaching to the converted and not building a coalition of support.

✌

Let's go back to consider Janet Rich at the pharmaceutical firm. Janet identified three key people from whom she'd like to get initial support. One of them was Darryl Wu, a chief scientist at the firm. While Darryl didn't develop the calcium-fortified gum, he had been pushing calcium fortification for years. Every time he had a chance, he shared with senior leaders the latest research on calcium deficiency problems in women and the lifestyle habits that exacerbated the problem.

In Darryl, Janet found a like-minded person who shared her passion for her idea and agenda. Janet had her initial support, but realized that the danger of having only Darryl on her side could lead others into thinking that she was simply seeking support from those who would reinforce her beliefs. She needed to use other mechanisms to expand her base of initial support to avoid the pitfall of being viewed as being in a cultish alliance with Darryl.

Co-opting Leaders

Jonathan Edwards, museum curator, and Roberta Jones, director of membership, are the most senior museum employees in terms of length of service. They have been with the museum since its founding seven years ago. Jonathan and Roberta embody all the traditions of the Deacon County Museum. Romi knew that getting them on board early could lead to a rapid mobilization of a coalition around his idea. They have organizational presence and therefore their initial support could quickly legitimize his intentions. But Romi also knew that in the event that they turn him down, especially publicly, his efforts to form a coalition would be jeopardized. He must co-opt them, and co-opt them privately.

Jonathan Edwards is an influential leader, but is also pursuing a Traditionalist agenda. He won't be easily swayed by Romi's arguments to tighten the museum's belt and to overhaul the way things were done at the Deacon. Roberta Jones has a similar way of thinking. Romi knew that co-opting either one of them would be a huge challenge, but with a potentially huge payoff. After much thought, Romi decided that he was more likely to engage Roberta with his agenda than Jonathan. In the short term, Romi would try to co-opt both of the museum's senior members.

ৡ

Co-opting leaders focuses on getting initial support of individual group leaders. The individual pushing the idea identifies key interest groups, but places the emphasis on persuading the leadership of the group—by identifying the specific interest of the leaders with the intention that the group they represent will follow. Co-opting has the potential for being the most attractive way of getting initial coalition support.

There are two problems with the strategy of co-opting. The first is that support from the leader of the group does not necessarily guarantee support from the entire group. You are effectively transferring the responsibility of selling your idea from you to the group leader. In many cases, the group will follow the leader's preferences, but you need to carefully gauge the probability of this happening before committing to this strategy. The second problem is that it may take time for the leader to negotiate the support of his or her constituents. There is nothing more dangerous to you than to think that you have the support of an interest group, only to find out later that you only have the leader of that group's blessing, but little tangible support from the members.

ॐ

Janet Rich seemed to have the initial support of like-minded Darryl Wu. But her next target, Sarah McCloskey, was much more of a challenge. Sarah was a category manager for the consumer products division. She wielded a tremendous amount of clout in the organization and if Janet could get her on board for this initiative, she'd have an important ally who could help mobilize a strong coalition. Janet worked on a buttoned-down presentation for the better part of a month—getting great feedback from her boss, from some colleagues who had dealt with McCloskey before, and from people outside the organization she admired. Her presentation focused on one major issue—the fact that the company had been unable to sell the chewing gum division and now needed to turn it around. Rather than offering me-too products, why not introduce a product that could stand alone on the shelf?

Janet scheduled a meeting and gave it her best shot. She had a forty-five-minute discussion with Sarah—about thirty minutes more than most people get with Sarah—and she left with Sarah's interest. Although McCloskey hadn't committed to do anything for Janet, it was clear that she was going to be supportive and open to taking action, as the need arose. Janet was on her way to a solid coalition.

Incorporating Groups

A third strategy for getting initial support is to identify groups and invite all members to participate in the coalition. This strategy provides the greatest promise for developing critical mass early on in your project. With relatively few groups, the change leader can muster the support needed to push the change initiative through the political machinery of the organization.

This strategy is employed frequently in public politics. Politicians seeking election will address large groups of voters (e.g., schoolteachers, Italian-Americans, religious congregations) as a way of building broad coalitions.

ॐ

Romi had another option. Rather than spending time in closed-door meetings, one-on-one lunches, and late-evening phone conversations, he began considering the option of addressing the museum staff at a large group meeting. He knew that by going this route of incorporating large groups, he could get his message out in a way that people would hear it from him, and not a filtered version that their bosses or coworkers might give them. Romi also knew that by addressing everyone at once, he might be able to identify those passionate people whose voices rarely get heard.

But Romi knew that going this route in getting initial support was potentially dangerous. What if the staff hated his ideas? What if he didn't really know how to best present his case to them? What would happen if Romi's directors saw this as doing an end run around them and diluting their power? He wrestled with this strategic decision for a solid week. He felt the clock ticking and saw the law of large numbers in this strategy.

In order to get initial support from the entire staff, he decided to address the entire museum staff as a whole at the end-of-the-month staff meeting. Romi planned to set up sub-committees to discuss his change agenda. He wanted to be open, democratic, and completely inclusive in establishing his coalition, believing that candor with everyone will ensure their participation. Romi thought, "Can I really pull this off? I've never been very good at speaking in front of an entire staff. I've never really had to do this."

❧

The problem with the strategy of incorporating groups is that it may take a long time for you to negotiate support, and the support may be flimsy. Leaders of groups tend to hold to their commitments, but the level of dedication of members of an entire group is hard to measure. The previous tactics, utilizing like minds and co-opting leaders, have the distinct advantage of being based on your ability to persuade a single individual at a time. In this case, you have to persuade an entire group. When using the other strategies, you rely on others to get the message out by either infiltrating the group or carrying out the message to the group as a whole. When using the incorporating strategy, you target everyone at once.

There is a certain attraction to this approach, but the pitfall is that groups can be fickle—as there is usually not one person who speaks on behalf of everyone. There is power in numbers, but that power can evaporate due to adverse circumstances or the focused efforts of your resistors. In getting initial support when you try to incorporate groups, you may unintentionally create a number of resistance subgroups.

There may be situations where you require public or group support early on. In those cases, you will have to rely on this strategy to succeed; however, if you really need a solid core of committed support, often incorporating groups is not the best enlistment strategy right out of the gate.

∽

Hollandale Department Store thrived on the upscale west side of the city for many years. It was very much a family business. The relationship of the Hollandale family, who saw themselves as part of the west-side community, with the workers had always been amicable and congenial. Because of the recent recession, Fred Hollandale came to the conclusion that he would have to cut the staff of the furniture and housewares departments. He thought it was most appropriate to address all sixty-three of his employees at once, informing them of the state of the store. He also decided to launch an employee committee to deal with the crisis. Unfortunately, what emerged was a center of resistance. The committee continued to meet for weeks and weeks to ponder this issue without taking action. More and more, the workers began to resent the situation they found themselves in.

Would Fred Hollandale have been better off either first identifying like-minded individuals or co-opting leaders before trying to incorporate the entire group as a whole? Certainly with an issue of this magnitude, he may have wanted to pursue a different tactic for initiating the change coalition.

In forming a coalition, it may be beneficial to use all of these strategies at once to get initial support. This can be tricky. If you begin with trying to get the initial support from people who have like minds, you may be accused of creating a cult or cabal. If you begin with seeking early support by co-opting leaders of key interest groups, you may be seen as engaging in collusion. If you begin by trying to enlist a whole group, you may be seen as grandstanding.

Each of the three strategies for getting initial support has advantages and disadvantages. Political competence necessitates that you evaluate which one you use and when you should use it in the context of your own unique situation. What is important is that you keep in mind that you have an array of strategies to choose from in order to get initial support.

Chapter 8

Justify Your Action

Jerome Claywar was an imposing figure at the Bard Elementary School. As principal, he needed to act every bit as big as his corpulent frame. The Bard School, a public school in the heart of a major city, was one of the most overcrowded schools in the nation. But there weren't many options for students or parents. Despite its large size, the Bard School had never lagged behind other city schools in test scores or student achievement, but it was not outstanding either. Claywar could be called a hero just for keeping student attendance at an acceptable level. With each grade having six classrooms of thirty-two kids, the Bard School resembled a small university as much as it did an elementary school.

But Jerome had had enough. After fifteen years of battling the system and trying to achieve incremental improvements and attracting incrementally more resources, he was ready to take a radical step. He read a lot about small school initiatives and the research showing how small schools outperformed behemoths like Bard across almost every category, and this inspired him to move beyond catfights over budgets for pencils and crayons and seek a more fundamental change. Jerome decided to push to split up Bard and try to create three separate elementary schools within his sprawling district.

Jerome had done his homework; detailed his initiative; socialized it among friends, colleagues, and confidants; and identified the key stakeholders. He evaluated their political agendas, relative to his Developer agenda. (Even though his idea may seem revolutionary, a Revolutionary agenda entails improvising, while Jerome's approach is definitely planning.) Now began the difficult challenge of getting real support. Jerome had a reservoir of tremendous respect throughout the community, within the city's public school system, and among politicians. Despite criticism from the teacher's union for not lobbying hard enough for resources and for their safety, he was a "teacher's principal" in that he was very hands-off when it came to letting the teachers run their classrooms. And he was criticized generally for his tendency to be insensitive to parents' and school board concerns. All in all, though, Jerome Claywar was the real deal.

Specifically, Jerome identified four people from whom he absolutely wanted—and needed—support: (1) Jerry Mayfield, the superintendent of the city public school system; (2) Malik Caster, president of the PTA; (3) Eileen Markley, head of the teacher's union; and (4) Celeste Ribino, city councilwoman for

Bard's school district. If he could get support from all of them, he'd consider himself a miracle worker. If he didn't get support from at least three, he'd never get such a politically charged initiative off the ground.

∽

You've developed some personal credibility, and you've identified the people you will try to get support from first. Now you have to justify to your potential allies the need for action. You have to persuade them that there is a need for action. To do this, you are going to have to prove the timeliness of your ideas. This is going to be a question of carefully selecting the best scenario to convince your targets for initial support that the time has come to act.

In trying to enlist people to join you in your effort, you should consider the four scenarios that you can use in making your case: rational, mimicking, regulation, and standards/expectations.*

---

* Some of these scenarios are based on research that was done on how organizations adapt to their environment. Do they rationally adapt to the environment? Do they mimic the environment? Or do they react to professional standards and expectations. This research can be found in the works of organizational behaviorists, known as neo-institutionalists, such as Walter W. Powell and Paul J. DiMaggio (*The New Institutionalism in Organizational Analysis,* University of Chicago Press, 1991).

The Rational Scenario: "Look at the numbers"

By using a rational scenario, you present a logical justification for change. Implicit in this argument for action is the assumption that you've arrived at the decision to take action through careful analysis, detailed cost-and-benefit projections, and a well-structured presentation of alternatives. You look at the numbers as they relate to money, time, and resources.

A rational scenario is calculated. You have to quantify both the costs and the benefits, and then subtract costs from benefits. If the benefits outweigh the costs, then you have a good reason for taking action. A rational scenario emphasizes the payoff to the organization, whether it takes the form of additional profits, a lower cost structure, or superior market position. You propose voluntary action based on sound data and logical projection.

Consider a decision to establish an employee assistance program (EAP) at a large consumer products firm. A rational scenario relies on market research and data, collected by an independent consulting firm, which reports that company employees miss, on average, ten days of work per year due to personal or mental health problems. You calculate, based on the average salaries in this 1,000-person organization, that those ten days of work (per employee) cost the organization a total of approximately $3 million per year. Further, you note that EAP vendors charge, on average, $500 per employee per year for an array of counseling and support services. You run the numbers and find that the EAP has a net benefit to the organization of $2.5 million per year. Who could argue with such logic? This is the basis of a rational scenario.

There may be a strong contingent of people who disagree with the rational scenario. They will challenge your assumptions. In the case of the EAP, critics may question whether the organization's experience with work loss due to mental health reasons mirror those of the average organization. Others may pick apart the average salary calculation for the organization. Still others may suggest that there are substantial hidden costs that you omitted in making the calculation.

There is usually not enough information, resources, or time to gather every last bit of data or conduct all of the analysis necessary to solidify an argument. In most cases, there are unquantifiable or subjective costs. Lastly, there's sometimes a difference between the magnitude of the numbers and the meaning of the numbers. Certain costs may not be significant in dollar terms but are strategically important.

You may be most successful in using a rational scenario— "Look at the numbers"—to call for action in an organization with a strong planning culture or firms where rigorous quantitative analysis is required before any decision is made. It may not work as well for you in mission-driven organizations—where qualitative factors often play as important a role as numbers. The rational scenario may falter in highly changeable situations where projections of future costs and benefits are difficult to quantify with any degree of accuracy—such as any initiative that relies on a forecast of the company's stock price. In highly volatile times, a rational scenario is much less persuasive.

❧

Jerome Claywar knocked on Jerry Mayfield's door. The superintendent's school office looked more like that of a *Fortune* 500 CEO than that of an educator. "Perhaps he earned it, surviving this mess of a school system for as long as he has," thought Claywar. He sat down on the leather sofa, adjacent to Mayfield's regal chair, and began his presentation.

Jerome started with the research on small schools. "Jerry, studies show that the average test scores, degree attainment, and emotional intelligence are all significantly higher in small schools than in larger schools. This research has been well supported by similar studies and also proven in longitudinal studies. It's time we pay attention to the data and take some action."

After a lengthy discussion about small school initiatives in other cities, Jerome broadened the discussion. "It's not just about academics, either. I've done an analysis of total operating costs for Bard and it is frightening. Based on discussions with real estate experts, estimates from the utility company, and estimates from our bus operators, I've determined that we could actually reduce the total operating costs of running three smaller schools by nearly 15 percent. Especially after you take into account the exorbitant maintenance and repair budget that Bard requires. Not only does this make academic sense, Jerry, but it makes fiscal sense!"

Later in the conversation, Jerome left Mayfield with one last bit of data. "And, Jerry, I don't need to remind you of the research done last year by the city that showed that 65 percent

of parents would like an overhaul of our school districting."
Jerome Claywar had made his case. He waited for Jerry Mayfield's reaction.

The Mimicking Scenario: "Everyone's doing it"

"Best-practice companies have adopted this approach to [fill in
the blank]." This is a classic mimicking scenario for action. Where
the rational scenario uses hard facts and logic, the mimicking
scenario relies on visibility to reduce the perceived risk of the
change initiative and to improve its legitimacy—"Organizations
do this, so we should too." The everyone's-doing-it argument
may seem simplistic, but it is often a sensible response, especially
in those instances when you don't have the time or resources to
experiment with an array of alternatives. Why not hitch your
wagon to what appears to be a successful best practice?

Sometimes, mimickers will identify processes of key competitors for replication. Other times, mimickers will choose
other organizations that have achieved best-in-class status for
certain processes. Think about how many service organizations
have copied Disney's customer service processes and training
as the gold standard for their own dissimilar industries.

The downside of mimicking is that in the context of
uncertainty, it's not clear what goals, products, technologies,
structures, and processes are most appropriate for any given
organization. As a result, many organizations often end up
adopting a change by simply copying it, without any concept

of its appropriateness or effectiveness. This goes a long way to explain organizational fads and fashions (e.g., re-engineering, zero-based budgeting, job enrichment).

The mimicking scenario is an easy target for critics. Some will call the initiative being promoted unimaginative. Others may thwart a mimicking scenario by examining the mimicked company's stock performance. For example, how many organizations pointed to Enron as a best-practice company for processes from innovation to business reinvention? Or how many cited Xerox's R&D activity as a best-in-class process? Even though Xerox's R&D activity may be impressive, critics may point to the beating the company's stock has taken over the last few years and ask, "Why would anyone want to mirror that performance?"

The mimicking scenario—"everyone's doing it"—may work best for you in larger organizations and in planning-oriented environments. Larger organizations are more likely to feel an affiliation with other large, best-practice companies. Smaller firms rarely compare themselves to large organizations and value originality more. If you choose a Traditionalist or a Developer agenda, you may prefer to use mimicking as a justification for adopting a change strategy, as this justification has a visible end-point as a target—making it possible to plan.

❧

Jerome Claywar stood up at the podium in the Bard School auditorium. He had never seen a PTA meeting so packed in his entire tenure at Bard. There must have been 250 parents or more. He fumbled around, started off awkwardly with a joke, and then launched into his speech and presentation.

Jerome started off with an overview of the benefits of small schools, but very quickly he shifted his argument.

"It is important to understand, though, that the move toward small schools is a trend, and we are falling behind. Chicago has moved toward small schools. Houston has a small school initiative now. California has been very successful with its efforts. Even Nashville is well down the road on a small school initiative. It is time for us to take notice and take action!"

The parents erupted in cheers.

"Now, let me take you through the successes of each of these urban public school systems. I think you'll find, as I did, that we need to keep up with other cities like ours. We cannot afford to fall lower in ranks—it is bad for the city and it is bad for our kids. So, I urge you to support a move to divide up Bard into three small schools. It has been successful in other cities far larger than ours and it will be successful in ours. Let's not fall further behind."

Jerome left the PTA meeting feeling like a hero. But did he convince the president of the PTA, Malik Caster?

The Regulation Scenario: "They made us do it"

Laws or regulatory changes occasionally require an organization to change its processes and/or the way it operates.

Consider how units within a telecommunications provider needed to change when the government lifted restrictions on providing local and long-distance service. There are plenty of organizations that use regulation as a reason for change.

With a regulation scenario, there is a strong third-party mandate for change. It is not difficult for you to obtain information about rules and regulations particular to an industry to determine whether the regulations actually require changing operations. Though not always quantifiable, regulations are nearly always accompanied by a body of written documentation that can be easily accessed and cited when necessary.

Regulations are not always clear—and they are subject to interpretation. Regulation-driven change frequently is tied to a time frame for compliance. People may say, "We don't have to comply with that for another four years," just as a way of delaying the change effort.

As an example, consider one women's clothing and accessory manufacturer with a very stable record of growth in Europe over the previous five years. Great Britain, Italy, and Germany are three of its five largest global markets. In each of those countries, it has implemented different, local strategies that have become quite successful.

With the creation of the European Union (EU), customer databases and privacy issues have come under scrutiny. The EU gradually is introducing regulations to standardize the law concerning how customer databases can and cannot be used. The worldwide marketing director determines that the way the clothing firm markets and generates list revenues will be radically altered. In some cases, the firm will lose an income stream. The marketing director needs to drive change through a successful organization that hasn't yet grasped the implications of the proposed legislation.

The marketing director will most likely draw on a regulation justification for the changes he wants to make in the division. He will collect news stories and analyses to support his argument. He may even procure the official minutes from EU meetings outlining the proposed regulations.

His staff may not understand the complexities of the EU and how the new rules apply to Italy. Others in the organization may see the legal ramifications as only arriving down the road, so their sense of urgency is reduced and their interest in staving off change is heightened.

In order to overcome the noninvolvement of others, the marketing director can introduce a rational scenario that indicates how much it would cost to implement a plan similar to his in five or ten years' time. Or he can research how other clothing manufacturers are dealing with the change in the laws and present a mimicking scenario. Just because the first scenario is rejected, doesn't mean that the push for creating a coalition is over.

You may find that the regulation scenario—"they made us do it"—has limits. Acquiescence to regulation and pressure does not mean that the organization becomes more effective. Rather, submitting to regulation may bring the organization into compliance with external governmental pressures, but it doesn't necessarily mean that compliance serves the efficiency of the organization. Many industries may see regulatory changes once every decade, while changes in their business take place annually or every couple of years.

$$\mathcal{L}$$

Jerome Claywar knew his biggest challenge was getting the support of the teacher's union. If Jerome had any enemy in the school system, it was most certainly the union. It wasn't a bitter relationship, but there was always tension and a general distrust of each other's intentions. Not surprisingly, the teacher's union saw Jerome's small school initiative as an attempt to "divide and conquer" the union. Jerome thought such an assumption was unfounded and countered in private conversations that the union was more interested in preserving itself than improving the school system.

Jerome came into the meeting with Eileen Markley, the head of the teacher's union, prepared for a war. But even though he was ready, he tried a tack that might convince Eileen that he and the union were on the same side on this one. He used the across-the-board budget cut that the city had implemented as the touchstone for the union's and for Jerome's problem. Jerome's strategy and message with Eileen was simple: The city—and their mandated budget cuts—did this to both of us.

"Eileen, how many years have we sat around complaining about the size of our classroom enrollments? And how many times have we—on separate and the same occasions—gone to the mayor and to school board officials? Our city has cut school budgets, allowed enrollments to increase, and prevented any kind of new districting or new building in town. We have been put in this untenable situation through years of neglect and bureaucracy.

"It's clear to me that the city-mandated budget cuts put us in this situation. They are making us fail! We've got to respond positively and in a unified way. It's time things change and the two of us can drive the changes we need to make. What do you think?"

The Standards/Expectations Scenario: "People expect it of us"

Sometimes you may want to justify the need to take action on the basis of normative expectation. *What would the community expect of us as an organization? What would the customers expect of us? What would our colleagues—constituency—international allies—expect of us?* When justifying action on the basis of the standards/expectations scenario, you are purporting to act in concert with the expectations of the greater community. While you may recognize that in the short term, this may not be beneficial to the bottom line, you believe that taking action that meets community expectations will have long-term benefits, such as customer loyalty, community trust, etc.

Regulation provides an explicit measure to justify change, while standards or external expectations provide implicit reasons for change. When you use the standards/expectations scenario as a reason for legitimizing your efforts, you are not proposing that the organization has to do something, as much as you are suggesting that if the organization doesn't do something, the organization will be at a disadvantage. Or, that if the organization does act, good things are likely to happen as a result.

∝

Baskerville Medical Center operates in a midsized U.S. city where it coexists with two teaching hospitals (both affiliated with major universities) and two other hospitals. One of the competing research hospitals has just upgraded its critical care facility—using state-of-the-art technology and a triage system that has both reduced the time that it takes to respond to a patient's trauma and improved the ability to diagnose problems.

Alice Barker, the head of Baskerville's critical care unit, is putting together a proposal to overhaul its facility so that it will compare favorably with its competitor. She plans on using the competitor's improved quality as the standard that Baskerville needs to meet.

When she makes her case to the senior management committee, she will try to show how the citizens of Baskerville have come to expect a higher quality of service and critical care than Baskerville Medical Center is offering today. The fact that the competition is meeting this standard makes the mandate for change even more compelling. She will argue that if Baskerville does not build a new critical care facility, it will fail to meet its community's raised sense of standards and the quality of service.

By focusing on standards and expectations, Alice uses a common justification. Standards and expectations arguments are particularly effective in organizations that provide premium quality products and services. It is also a common justification for change in institutions of higher education and in health and governmental organizations—where success is more often defined in highly qualitative terms, rather than financial terms.

In the public sector, government factions perpetually try to justify taking action as a means of addressing the needs of others with standards and expectations arguments. Officials seek the high ground of moral justification and maintain that their actions are predicated on the very expectations of the public. For example, for a government to eliminate poverty or provide security allows the initiator of the action to say, "I am doing this because it is expected."

∼

The City Council's office isn't always the most comfortable place to have a meeting, but Jerome Claywar knew that he had to go to Celeste Ribino's home turf in order to push his idea ahead. It took him four months just to get on Celeste's calendar. He knew he'd be lucky to get fifteen minutes of her undivided attention.

So, Jerome cut straight to the chase. "Councilwoman Ribino, I've been in this school district for over twenty-three years. And for the better part of the past decade, we have seen a huge increase in the demands of families on the quality of education in public schools. We have seen our nation's major cities go through restructuring and reinvention of their public school systems. Safe to say, there isn't a politician in any city—including you—who doesn't have education high on their agenda for the next election. Our community expects a higher quality education system from us. People are expecting more from public school education. And the bottom line, Councilwoman, is that we're not meeting those expectations—and it's time we start."

Celeste was taken aback by Jerome's direct and somewhat critical comments. She followed up with, "Mr. Claywar, with all due respect, since I have been in office, we have increased public school budgets more than at any other time in history."

"Fair enough," Jerome continued, "but those budget increases have taken the form of very tactical moves. Putting plugs in leaks, rather than redoing the plumbing. I'll be the first to admit that I've benefited from your strong efforts here in city hall. However, we've gotten to where our schools are at the saturation point and have a limited capacity to improve. The system is broken and the public knows it. Their standards for their children's education needs have risen over the past decade. But we have not changed the standard to which we teach! There is a wider disconnect between what our community expects and what we are delivering. And, now, they are starting to get more restless and angrier in a way that can no longer be addressed by continuing to tweak budgets."

"So, what do you propose, Mr. Claywar?"

"As mentioned in my e-mails, there's an opportunity to totally transform the way our community views public education and to increase the quality of education that the public school students in your district receive. By splitting the district into three distinct public schools, rather than the one behemoth we have, we will rise to the expectations that our community has for us—and to the high levels of quality that, frankly, we should be holding ourselves to. I need your active support in making this a reality. And I urge you not just for selfish reasons. This is an opportunity for you to be a leader in urban public school education and to show the taxpayers why their votes for you were absolutely justified."

"I've got a lot of questions that need to be answered before I'll commit to backing your proposal," Celeste replied. "At first glance, there seem to be some pretty fundamental issues, not least of which being the financial implications of what you are proposing."

"Councilwoman, I am prepared to take you through the details of my plan. You'll see how we can deliver a program that will meet the expectations our community's parents have for their children's education."

Taking Stock

Mobilizing a coalition is all about your ability to gain legitimacy—within and beyond the organization. People want to get behind an idea or a person who is going to win or, at the very least, is not going to look like a loser. This early stage in coalition building is all about establishing your credibility and building the case that will move others to support your effort. Think of it as a foundation on which you are going to build your initiative. Without a base of support, it is unlikely that you'll ever develop a strong enough critical mass to push your initiative through.

You now know that personal credibility comes from a combination of four dimensions: your authoritative position, your personal integrity, your expertise and knowledge, and the specific time and opportunity when you act. While you don't need to be strong in all four dimensions, you must have at least one where your credibility is clear to others. If anyone has to question your credibility, it is unlikely that they will support your effort. Think about courtroom testimony. When the prosecution calls a witness, one of the first things the defense will try to do is to impugn the witness's credibility. So goes the resistance to any kind of change effort. Anyone you approach for support will first ask herself, "Why would I back this particular person?" You need to have an answer to that question, and you hope that, it is clear enough that you don't even have to answer it.

Even with personal credibility, you will still need to persuade your potential supporters. That means choosing the right strategy to get them on board and to justify the effort in their own minds.

Choosing the right strategy for gaining potential supporters involves one of three approaches. You can try to utilize like minds, co-opt specific leaders, or incorporate groups. To choose the right strategy, you'll need to carefully consider the people you are seeking support from, their role or position in the organization, or the people they influence.

Once you've gotten meetings with the people you need to get behind you, you need to make the right pitches. Are your prospective supporters rational, data-driven people? Or are they concerned with best practices? You need to tailor each argument to address the concerns of your prospective supporter. Your success—especially early on—will depend on choosing the appropriate scenario.

If you've done your homework right and executed it well, you should now have initial support for your coalition and focus on getting the actual buy-in.

Part III

Make Things Happen

Chapter 9

Get the Buy-In

You have your initial support. Your challenge is to effectively persuade skeptics and potential allies to join your coalition. You have to go beyond getting initial support to get them to buy in to the coalition. Getting initial support is getting them to listen and to reflect. Getting the buy-in is taking it one step further in getting them on your side. While initial support has to do with identifying allies and resistors and explaining your position, getting the buy-in has to with negotiating and persuading them to join your efforts. In getting the buy-in, you must tap the motivation of allies, potential allies, and resistors. You have to discern their potential motivation for joining you in this effort and communicate that to them. You have to be specific about the practical benefits they will gain by joining your effort.

Economists and social psychologists maintain that this means you have to communicate in terms of the subjective expected utility of others.* Subjective expected utility is nothing more than figuring out what option has the best chance of giving you what you want. In other words, individuals will often decide whether to join a coalition by asking themselves, "What's in it for me?" They compare what they will gain by joining the coalition versus what they will gain by staying outside of the coalition. Subjective expected utility implies that people will compare the magnitude of the potential payoff of working within a coalition to the magnitude of the potential payoff of working outside of a coalition.

Consider the decision of James and Ellen to marry. What was their decision to get married about? It was about happiness—the most subjective constant in human life. Ask anyone why they marry and they will say, "We'll be happier married than unmarried." A married couple forms a coalition because they feel that by operating together they can achieve collective happiness. They each could achieve a greater degree of happiness together than they could by staying single.

In terms of the subjective-expected-utility theory, what ran through their minds? Essentially, James and Ellen asked themselves the following: "If I marry this person, what is the magnitude of happiness I can expect to achieve? How does this compare to the happiness I could achieve alone or with

* See, for example, J. von Neumann and O. Morgenstern, *Theory of Games and Economic Behavior* (2nd ed.) (Princeton University Press, 1947: original work published 1944). See also Jon Elster, *Rational Choice (Readings in Social & Political Theory)* (New York University Press, 1986).

some other spouse? If I live alone, I can do whatever I want, I'd have more money, and I'd have more time to self-reflect. If I got married, I'd have less loneliness, someone to worry about me, and someone to help me grow."

Discussing the decision to marry as similar to a business decision may be comparing apples and oranges, but we all create this subjective fiction of the magnitude of happiness to help us visualize what it is that we can achieve.

James may ask himself, "What is the probability that I can achieve this magnitude of happiness married to Ellen? What is the probability that I would have achieved this happiness married to Sylvia, my former girlfriend? Ellen does have certain drawbacks. It is not 100 percent guaranteed that I'll achieve this level of happiness, but on the other hand, do I have a better shot trying to achieve it on my own or by marrying someone like that woman at the gym, whom I think about from time to time, but know very little about."

This is how someone subjectively evaluates the benefits of joining or not joining a coalition. James decided what the magnitude of the payoff—in this case, happiness—was and evaluated the probability of his achieving it with Ellen.

In trying to get buy-in to your coalition, you have to make sure you address what your resistors and potential allies believe are the benefits in joining your coalition. You have to make it clear that there is a payoff in supporting your effort and that there are possible drawbacks for not joining your coalition.

Consider the instance where individuals have very similar agendas. For two managers pursuing Traditionalist agendas—

as it relates to the organizational culture—joining a coalition opposing organizational change for them would be seen as a very integrative effort. There would be a positive payoff for both of them. Similarly, those with Adjuster agendas and those with Traditionalist agendas would join the same coalition, each making concessions but agreeing that a coalition is beneficial to both parties. On the other hand, consider a Traditionalist agenda confronting a Revolutionary agenda. It is unlikely that either could see much to gain from joining the same coalition. They can only gain at the other's expense.

In getting buy-in, your challenge is to persuade resistors and potential allies that their support for your effort is beneficial to them.* In this context, you have three tactical decisions:

1. Do you want to approach resistors and potential allies tacitly or explicitly?
2. Do you want to talk in broad principles or specifics?
3. Do you want to talk about a single issue or multiple issues?

Your answers to these three questions will have a profound impact on your ability to build an effective coalition and on the type of coalition you'll eventually build.

---

* For a detailed discussion of the importance of coalition mobilization and buy-in in organizations, see S. B. Bacharach and E. J. Lawler, *Power and Politics in Organizations*, Jossey-Bass, 1980.

Tacit vs. Explicit Persuasion

There are two styles of persuasion. The first is the informal, indirect, tacit approach and the second is the head-on, formal, explicit approach.* A tacit approach has the subtlety of an informal afterthought, a side conversation, a by-the-way mentality. An explicit approach is thought out in advance, and the main focus of a conversation.

When you are communicating tacitly, you are probing. You feel out your resistors and potential allies and test where they stand vis-à-vis the issues you've raised. When forming a coalition, tacit communication tends to be simple water-cooler conversations, the casual drop-in, or the discussion at the delegates' dining table at the United Nations.

Sometimes the water cooler just won't do. Sometimes when getting the initial buy-in, you have to put the issues on the table. You have to persuade others head-on. You have to leave the informality of the delegates' dining room and sit down at the Security Council table and put your cards down. You have to explain to your resistors and potential allies that you want their buy-in. You explicitly negotiate coalition membership.

Consider how an R&D team leader tells the chief scientist that his pet project is going in the wrong direction. The issue for the team leader is not only what to say, but how to say it. Does

---

* This distinction is based on Walton and McKersie's distinction between tacit and explicit bargaining in their book *A Behavioral Theory of Labor Negotiations* (McGraw Hill, 1965).

he drop subtle hints? Suggest it informally? Propose it boldly at a formal meeting? The team leader has to figure out the best way to approach the chief scientist. He decides that the best way to confront the chief scientist is tacitly. In this instance, if the team leader frames the negotiations explicitly and formally, the scientist may feel cornered. But, by catching him informally, the team leader can get a better sense of the chief scientist's priorities and willingness to negotiate. While tacit communication is not ideal for making quick decisions, it is enough for the team leader to get a sense of the malleability of the chief scientist in terms of altering the course of his pet project.

Informal, tacit persuasion reduces the chance that you'll be rejected. You won't lose points by having your invitation to join your coalition publicly rejected. Tacit communication requires subtlety and is often barely perceptible. You cast out a line and see if you get a nibble. In drawing people into your coalition it is sometimes better to be tacit, giving everyone the opportunity to climb down from the pole.

Formal, explicit persuasion, on the other hand, is essentially what nations, corporations, and unions do when they sit down at the bargaining table and exchange offers and counteroffers. When you sit at a table, you know that you are negotiating membership into a coalition. There is nothing subtle about it. When you are explicitly bargaining a coalition, you are sitting face-to-face, discussing, debating, and making proposals and counterproposals. When you are tacitly negotiating a coalition, much will depend on the social setting in which you choose to bargain.

Agreements to establish a coalition through explicit communication are more likely to be stable and also are apt to have built-in safeguards against a breach by either party. Tacit agreements are more likely to be ambiguous, unbinding, and unenforceable. By their very nature, tacit agreements can be broken with impunity and require a certain level of trust among all the parties involved in order for them to work successfully.

How to Negotiate a Change Coalition	
Tacit Persuasion	Explicit Persuasion
Gives Plausible Deniability	Forces the Issue
Establishes Informal Coalition	Establishes Formal Coalition
Avoids Spotlight	Creates Public Recognition
Establishes Unstated, but Understood, Exchanges	Establishes Understood and Stated Exchanges

You should use tacit persuasion to negotiate a coalition when you want to minimize the risk of public rejection and explicitly negotiate a coalition when you want to force the issue.

❧

Jeff Tyler, the HRIS (Human Resource Information System) director for Procter, Reed, and Cooper (PRC), a major fund management firm, had a problem. He had to convince the managing directors and human resource VPs of PRC's funds that it would be a good idea to centralize their separate payroll and HR data systems into one integrated, Web-based system. This system would enable directors and fund managers to perform all HR transactions—such as pay increases, promotions, and transfers—at their own desk through a Web-based portal into the centralized system, rather than having someone in HR fill out paper forms in triplicate and waiting two weeks for someone in payroll to manually enter that data into the system. It would also allow the users to see the data for their work forces online in real time through advanced Web-based reporting, rather than having to rely on someone in HR to manually produce a spreadsheet from payroll data every time the partner wanted to have a view of the current status of employee performance, salary history, and tenure. There would be significant savings by eliminating duplicate staff in payroll and human resources.

Jeff knew that this systems integration would deliver millions of dollars of savings to the firm, and finally bring it into the twenty-first century in terms of payroll technology and infrastructure—since PRC's current payroll and HR data processing were all housed on decades-old mainframe-based systems. Even better, in Jeff's mind, once the new system (dubbed

"HR Connect") was in place, the HR teams in the various divisions, who up until then had been spending half their time processing paper forms and tracking paper payroll printouts to manage personnel transactions in the businesses, would finally be freed up to do strategic HR work. This, he believed, would help drive improvements in the way the firm operated and in the way it hired and retained promising investment specialists. But Jeff was also politically competent enough to know that, even though he had some obvious allies, he'd also have a fair number of resistors to his idea.

Jeff thought about how he could move this idea forward. He considered going to each managing director and each VP-HR to try to build his coalition one by one. But Jeff was impatient and didn't want to wait. He also felt that if he went to each individually, he might not get the full commitment that he was seeking. Instead, Jeff decided that he'd bring the directors and the HR-VPs for each fund together and make his case in a "kickoff" meeting.

Jeff prepared carefully. He mastered the details of the system, mapped the process improvements it would deliver, and developed the case for the proposed change. He ran his presentation by a few colleagues in IT, who were very impressed with it.

The skeptics identified themselves quickly. First of all, the managing directors said to themselves, "Why should I give up control over my own payroll system and let some bureaucrats in corporate HR run it?" And furthermore, each partner thought, "I know I will be charged back a monstrous allocation fee from corporate if this system is implemented, and that would only bring further scrutiny over my unit's budget, which is tight enough as it is." As for the HR-VPs, self-preservation was the reason for their resistance: Each believed that if the day-to-day work of managing personnel transactions and payroll data disappeared, corporate would use that as a justification for reducing HR's head count, which would shrink the HR-VPs' power base and control.

Even more threatening, most HR-VPs (especially those with longer tenure) feared that with a new system in place to handle the HR transactional work, they would be expected to do more sophisticated and strategic HR work in their divisions, and most of them didn't even know the definition of "strategic HR work." With a new integrated system in place, they knew that the folks in corporate would have much greater HR data-reporting capabilities and would have much greater insight into what was going on in each of the units, such as: How many sign-on bonuses did HR approve each year? How much personnel turnover actually occurred each quarter?

Jeff chose an explicit approach to mobilizing his coalition and confronting skeptics. But, because of the concerns that the directors and the HR-VPs had with the change Jeff was proposing, and because Jeff did not consult one-on-one with each stakeholder first, the kickoff strategy-planning meeting for the new system was a disaster. When Jeff began his recitation of the benefits and cost savings of the proposed system, he was interrupted every two minutes by one director or HR-VP or another. One director piped up, "We don't believe your system can produce those savings—where did you get your numbers?"

One HR-VP interjected, "And how do we know that the new Web-based system can't be hacked into by outsiders who want to steal our personal data?" Others jumped on the bandwagon: "Our current systems produce paychecks just fine" . . . "You're threatening the stability of our work force management" . . . "Why do we need to change?" Also, "You're just looking to cram down a system that will make less work for HR and more work for managers—how does that help us improve earnings in our practice areas or at PRC as a whole?"

Jeff failed to account for one critical factor: By choosing an explicit approach to the negotiation, he effectively forced the directors and HR-VPs to make a decision at the meeting, causing a surge of political resistance. Furthermore, any allies or potential allies in that meeting were too intimidated to stand up and support Jeff in front of the highly influential camp of resistors.

Needless to say, after that initial meeting, Jeff had to regroup with his team and rethink the implementation strategy. Maybe, he thought, I need another approach to secure the support of our divisional CEOs and HR-VPs. And he was right: He needed a healthy dose of political competence to help him muddle through this major organizational change he was contemplating for the organization.

Talk on the Same Level as Others

Persuading people to buy in to your coalition is a question of language, expression, and the use of words. It is about negotiating with skeptics and persuading potential allies to share your intention, vision, and ambition. You want others to see your idea as you see it. In order to do this, you begin negotiating a coalition by viewing your proposed change from the perspective of those people you want to buy in. You should realize that people who share your agenda could be dissuaded from joining your coalition if you alienate them by not talking to them on the same level. It is critical when getting others to support you that you not talk past them—that you talk to them on the same level.

Some may view your proposal as being broad and ideological, and therefore, when considering whether to join you, they want to discuss subtle issues such as meaning, symbols, and understanding. Others may consider your idea as being very specific and only want to deal with nuts-and-bolts issues of how, what, where, and when. People in the former group want to discuss big strategic goals: What do we mean by culture? What is in the intent of the new structure? What is the intent of the new goals? The latter group wants to focus on the nitty-gritty specifics or tactical goals of how the coalition is going to get results.

Consider Israeli politics. All parties cannot agree on what they mean by the broad strategic goal of peace. Israeli parties on the right tend to see peace as an all-encompassing notion: exchanging of ambassadors, sharing in economic and cultural activities, etc. Other Israeli factions view peace as basically "live and let live"—a cold peace. One of the fundamental problems in Israel's ability to bring about change is how to build a coalition based on these conflicting notions of peace: Can there really be peace between Israel and Egypt, and how is that different from the peace that exists between Israel and Jordan? Is the fact that there is no aggression between Israel and Egypt enough to connote peace? Or does peace imply more, like a cultural exchange of ideas and daily commerce? Does peace imply genuine, mutual respect? Or a grudging, hands-off approach?

Ideally, in trying to persuade others to join your coalition, you should deal with broad strategic issues first and then work out the nuts-and-bolts details. It may be the case that while you talk about broad, strategic issues, your colleagues want to discuss nuts-and-bolts tactical issues. For example, you may speak of the vision of peace while others talk about such issues as, "Where will the line of demarcation between Palestine and Israel be?" "Where will the bridge crossing be?" "How will the Israeli monetary system be tied to the Palestinian monetary system?" "How will monitoring for weapons be conducted?" "Who will ensure access to ports?" "How will issues of jurisdiction be handled?" As a result, everyone talks past each other.

Establishing broad strategic consensus may be difficult. Instead, you may find it easier to begin the dialogue by addressing specific nuts-and-bolts tactical issues. If you want your coalition to have the support of people who strategically object to your position, you are going to have to persuade them with tactical arguments. By first resolving some key nuts-and-bolts details, you will lead everyone to reach a level of trust and understanding that will result in a broad strategic consensus.

Rather than being caught in the continuous debate over the broad issue of "peace," if Israeli and Palestinian leaders could negotiate the nuts-and-bolts of a shared industrial zone, this could possibly be the first step toward a common notion of peace. Broad strategic consensus can emerge from a nuts-and-bolts discussion. Sometimes it may be the case that, as it is said in the movie *Field of Dreams*, "If you build it, they will come."

When resistors and potential allies make nuts-and-bolts tactical arguments, you have an opportunity to persuade them on a line-by-line basis. When dealing with specific issues, you'll be able to lay out your position and make tangible arguments. When talking specifics of where to put a border crossing or how to redesign the assembly line, you can have a relatively concrete discussion over the pros and cons of the technologies of implementation. To a certain degree, the discussion is self-evident. It is likely that people who debate on concrete issues may see room for compromise and are strong potential candidates for your growing coalition.

Adjusters, who prefer to pick up cues from the environment, and those choosing a Developer agenda, regard change as being an incremental process, and are most likely to keep the negotiations for joining a coalition in the realm of nuts and bolts. Traditionalist and Revolutionary agendas are inclined to make broad strategic arguments based on principle. Mobilizing a coalition will depend on your ability to make sure that everyone is talking on the same level.

❧

Jeff Tyler walked into Melinda Kennedy's office, five minutes early for his three o'clock meeting. He felt confident and decided that Melinda needed to understand the specifics of his proposal, rather than the broad ideology or principles. He and Melinda shared some small talk about the numbers that the company reported earlier that day and speculated about the managing partner's comment about needing "new capabilities to compete." After that icebreaker, Jeff made his case.

"Melinda, I know you weren't comfortable with the way the last meeting went, so I went back and put a little something together that I thought might clarify some of the issues and address your concerns. If you have the time, it won't take more than half an hour."

Melinda agreed, and Jeff continued. "Well, Melinda, you raised the issue of security and information privacy at the last meeting. And I couldn't agree with you more. Let me show you how we're dealing with it. When Warren ran IT, he had us all on NT servers. They were really robust and interfaced nicely with our applications server and with our Web interface. The problem with them is that this new system uses ASPs for our Web interface and the NT servers have to use Active-X controls. These can create holes in our firewall, enabling hackers and unauthorized users to enter into the system.

"Under this new system that I'm proposing, we would migrate our systems architecture from an NT-based environment to a Unix-based environment. Yes, Unix is criticized as a legacy system by some, but the fact of the matter is that it can better handle the huge processing demands that this new system would place on it and it tends to offer a much more secure computing environment. No Active-X controls. And we can still implement that PKI that Warren wanted."

Melinda stared at Jeff, her eyes slightly glazed, thinking about how badly she needed a mocha latte right about now. Melinda said to herself, "Active what? I keep hearing these terms, but don't have a clue what they mean. When is Jeff going to come down the mountain and talk about the issues I really care about?" So, she continued her blank stare, while Jeff droned on.

"Are you following this?" he said. "It's really important because I think we're going to have to move to an LDAP so that employees have a more secure log-in to conform with the new security policies and standards. That may run us some money, but I think, with the right vendor, we can negotiate that into the system price. One of the open items remains Web access for remote employees. Because our security standard requires a dynamically generated IP address, we may have to provide each employee with an authentication device that dynamically generates a password. It is an extra procedure, but I think people will get used to it."

Jeff wrapped up, "So, Melinda, I hope you see that we have a really strong plan for dealing with security patches and ensuring that the new system will comply with our IT policies and standards. Any questions?"

"Jeff, it sounds like you've thought a lot about this and have something of a plan in place. Honestly, though, I have no idea what you've been talking about. My knowledge of computers stops with e-mail and URLs. I don't think you quite understand my concerns about security, and if you feel you've addressed them, I don't have a clue how you did. You've been talking about details this whole time. I'm interested in the big picture and its implications. Listen, I have to prepare for my four o'clock. Why don't we pick this up another time?"

Jeff may have squandered his chance of persuading an ally to join his coalition. Melinda seemed to be sympathetic to his cause—and Jeff seemed to be interested in being responsive to Melinda's security concerns. But Jeff chose to focus on specifics, rather than dealing with Melinda on broad principles. He turned a concern about security into a highly technical issue and discussion, while Melinda was thinking about it at a more strategic, less tactical level.

By not being sensitive to this, Jeff found himself talking at a different level than Melinda. Even if Melinda wanted to support Jeff, she couldn't because she couldn't understand his language. This is a common problem in organizations—particularly for initiatives that develop from more technical parts of the business.

∾

As a politically competent leader, you need to be sensitive to the language that others understand and use. You need to make sure that you avoid talking at a level that key stakeholders cannot understand. A politically competent leader deciphers whether resistors and potential allies are talking on a strategic or tactical level. If you are talking strategy while they are talking tactics, you will inevitably talk past each other.

Specify the Number of Issues

In presenting your initiative to potential coalition members you want to buy in to your idea, you have to determine whether you want them to coalesce around one issue or multiple issues. A single-issue approach treats an issue in isolation from other issues, whereas a multiple-issue approach stresses the packaging or grouping of issues.

Considering one issue in isolation has the advantage of allowing you to make concentrated arguments. The benefit of a single-issue approach is that you are able to make focused and detailed arguments, and not have your attention diverted by extraneous details. *How will the work be done? Who will be responsible for the communication network?* The advantage of dealing with only one issue is that it allows you to establish a narrow coalition that will hone in on a specific target. The drawback is that once you have achieved your narrow change goal, you will have to start all over from scratch when forming a new coalition for your next effort. Another disadvantage of a single-issue coalition is that it gives resistors and potential allies a choice of "either you are with us or against us."

Forcing the initial coalition to focus on one issue rather than multiple issues may enhance your ability to establish a strong, but narrow, coalition that will see you through a short-term change. Focusing on multiple issues allows you to create a broader, more diversified coalition.

Unlike the single-issue approach, the multiple-issue strategy lets you attract a broad range of interest in your coalition. Some of your proposals may get outright buy-in from a number of parties. Other ideas may only get you a partial buy-in. Your goal is to get as much interest in your coalition from as many people as possible. The advantage of having multiple issues is that it affords you the opportunity to establish a coalition that appears to be mutually beneficial to your potential allies.

How focused do you want to make your initial coalition efforts? If you focus on only one issue in the marketing division, what will it mean in the long term? You may have a successful coalition for short-term change, but in the long run, it may mean that you restrict your opportunity to expand your coalition to address a number of issues. If you focus on multiple issues, your coalition may be broad but unstable at the early stages of your effort, but, over time, your coalition has greater potential for creating action in the future.

What is your long-term ambition? If you seek focused, concentrated change, you should create your initial coalition on a single issue; if you want long-term, broad change and are willing to accept initial instability in the beginning, then you should mobilize a coalition based on multiple issues.

✍

Vivian Lo Porto was the VP-HR for the firm's intellectual property practice. She was reasonably supportive of Jeff's idea in his kickoff meeting, but mentioned to him after the meeting that she had some concerns that she'd like to discuss with him privately. He had no idea what they were, so he didn't prepare anything for his meeting with Vivian.

Vivian began her discussion with Jeff by talking about multiple issues, rather than simply Jeff's initiative. "Thanks for meeting with me, Jeff. Let me say, first off, you've got a great idea here. If we don't do this soon, we're really sacrificing long-term opportunities. So, I'm clearly behind what you want to do. But this raises other issues for me. I've got a relatively large staff in the comp area, whose jobs would become potentially redundant. Also, I'd need to get people trained to use this system and I just don't have the training budget today. We've had to cut back drastically, you know."

"Yeah, tell me about it! We've had the same problem," Jeff agreed, unaware that Vivian was signaling him that there was more than his initiative at stake for her.

"I also am going to have to deal with Peter [the partner in charge of the intellectual property practice] and his direct reports, none of whom will want to take on the administrative end of this HRIS. Since I've been pushing hard on implementing this performance management system, my line managers are pretty much up to here when it comes to taking on another initiative that requires additional administrative time on their end. They have a lot of trouble seeing the same benefits we see, Jeff. So, you have to understand that as helpful as I'd like to be, there's got to be a way that we can frame it in conjunction with these other priorities I have."

Jeff thought for a few seconds and then responded, with a continued disregard for Vivian's multiple-issue argument, "Yeah, I see what you mean. But let's just focus on the HRIS for now. I understand that you've got more on your plate than you can handle. But if we start confusing the issues, then we won't get anything accomplished. Anyway, you don't need to be going to Peter yet and we're a long way off before your comp people will feel any sort of squeeze. What I need is your support on the HRIS . . . and I think I have that, right?"

Vivian became more dismissive: "Well, I think it's a great idea and we'll eventually need to move toward something like that."

"Great, then we agree. I'll be talking to others over the next week or so and then come back with a follow-up meeting. In fact, I'll be meeting with Peter tomorrow."

"OK, Jeff. But just know that you're fighting an uphill battle with Peter. He's just trying to keep the practice afloat right now. We're in turnaround mode."

"Yeah, I know. Let's stay in touch on this."

Note how Vivian put Jeff's initiative in the context of a broader set of battles that she was fighting in the organization. She was making a multiple-issues argument, while Jeff chose to focus on a single-issue argument—his HRIS or not his HRIS. Even though Jeff saw his project as something that could be treated separately from other issues, Vivian might be forced to choose to support (or not to support) Jeff's initiative, relative to other competing agendas. If she needed to work well with Peter (her boss), it might not be in her best interest to support Jeff's agenda.

Though Jeff found it easier to make this a single issue, he needed the political competence to understand that others may not see it as a single issue. He may, indeed, have benefited from positioning it in the context of more than one issue. In this case, it would seem that Jeff would likely lose the support of Vivian—not because his initiative wasn't valuable, but because it was not valuable enough to Vivian.

Chapter 10

Put Your Ideas in Place

Think about a plant. At its early stages, its root system cannot support the aboveground growth, making the plant easy to uproot. As its roots take hold, they provide the foundation for the plant's stems to grow strong and full. Such is the dynamic of leading a coalition. At the early stages, a coalition is like the young plant—easy to uproot. But, as an effective leader, your challenge is to nourish a stronger root system, while you grow new leaves and branches, or rather, new coalition members.

Keep in mind that the main purpose for developing a coalition is to establish a base that will legitimize your ideas and provide a platform to push their ideas through the organization. While some view a coalition as the end, it is advisable to view the coalition as a means to ensure that your ideas are put in place in the organization.

So, you've successfully built initial support for your idea and you've gotten buy-in from a core coalition of supporters. Now you need to put your ideas in place. Specifically, you want to make sure that your ideas are a focus of consensus in your coalition, are adopted by others, and are diffused throughout the organization to the point where they become part of those things that your colleagues take for granted. You want to make sure that your ideas are no longer fragile suggestions or precarious hopes. You want your ideas to be part of the accepted culture of the organization. You don't want people to be constantly questioning new ideas, processes, or techniques. You want them to take them for granted. You want others to have a sense of ownership over the new ideas, processes, or techniques.

When you first suggest a new idea, it is natural for people to reflect on it and question it, but you want to go beyond getting the buy-in. You don't want people constantly questioning whether they should implement the idea, whether it is a good process or a good technique. You want your idea put in place. You want people to be reflexive, to take the idea for granted, rather than to be perpetually reflective. Your challenge is to move them from conscious, reflective evaluation that accompanies the initiation of a new idea to a more reflexive sense, which is necessary to get the idea in place, after you have the buy-in. How can you get your idea in place if your colleagues and fellow coalition members are constantly in evaluation mode while you still feel the need to justify your ideas? In the politics of organizations, people sometimes mistakenly think because they have the buy-in, then the idea is in place. This isn't true. Putting the idea in place requires that you effectively:

1. Solidify your coalition
2. Work out differences among members of the coalition
3. Diffuse and network

Until you are able to do these three things, you may have gotten some people on your side, but you're not going to be able to get results.

Solidify Your Coalition

Solidifying a coalition is the organizational equivalent of nurturing a plant during its formative stages. It is a key step in effectively leading your initiative. You solidify a coalition by ensuring that there is a sense of homogeneity among coalition members—that there is a common purpose shared by everyone.

In the beginning stages of your change effort, you may find that early supporters were really only supporters in casual conversation, or they were supporters up until the point that you went public with your agenda. Once you take your agenda out of the closet, sometimes those who you thought were solidly behind you run for cover. Risk-averse individuals see themselves as having too much to lose by supporting an untested and uncertain effort early on. They are enthusiastic about your idea only in the safety of private conversation. You will need to quickly weed out your dubious supporters, so that you don't find yourself with a stunted root system.

$$\mathcal{D}$$

Let's return to the Deacon County Museum of Contemporary Art. Romi Cruz met with Mia Stephens and Arnold Hynes, the two most recently hired curators, to try to build their commitment. Romi felt that since both were in a very similar position that he might be able to leverage their mutual interests. With the two curators in his camp, Romi felt he'd have enough critical mass to really begin to move his agenda forward.

Romi planted the seeds a couple of weeks ago. He bumped into Mia in the hall one day and she looked frustrated. As their conversation developed, Mia shared with Romi her disappointment that decisions were made so haphazardly that it made it difficult for her to develop a solid plan for the sculpture section of the museum. Romi lent a sympathetic ear and invited her and Arnold (through Mia) to lunch to discuss it further.

At lunch, after a little small talk about the museums where the two used to work, Romi cut to the chase. "I've been thinking about our conversation last week, Mia. And I really want to help the two of you. I think, with the proper positioning, we can make some targeted investments in the collections that you oversee. I'd really like to see both of you develop a direction for your collections that you can call your own. I know, though, by the way we've been operating, it is tough to see how that might happen. That's why I was hoping you might be able to give me some feedback on some ideas I've been batting around recently."

"Sure, Romi, we'd be happy to," agreed Mia.

"Yeah, what did you have in mind, Romi?"

"Well, as you know, this museum has experienced tremendous growth since its inception. Jonathan has done an incredible job of putting the museum's collection on the map as one of the most progressive and innovative in the country." Mia and Arnold cautiously nodded with approval, not knowing exactly where Romi was heading.

"Now, Jonathan needs your help." Mia and Arnold sat stoically, trying to read between the lines while assessing Romi's intentions. "He's moved the museum's collection in many interesting directions, but now needs your help in focusing it a bit more. What's more, Jonathan needs to build some consistency into his programs. Experimenting the way we do was fine when we were just getting started. But now people come to us for certain things and we need to make sure that we serve those interests. At the same time, we need to ensure that we stay on the forefront in areas where we can lead and, perhaps, let some of the other seeds we've planted take a more organic course."

Mia and Arnold understood the code for "Dump those collections!" Mia and Arnold wanted to enthusiastically support Romi's plan, but they viewed Romi's intentions with skepticism. They didn't want to give him the idea that they'd support something radical, like getting rid of Jonathan. Arnold broke the momentary silence. "Romi, how can we help?"

"Well, I'd like to get your feedback on some of the details of my plan before going to Jonathan."

"You know, Romi, we think Jonathan's doing a good job," Mia said, trying to assess Romi's intentions.

"Absolutely! I think he's a phenomenal curator. But in order to get to the next level of growth, we need more discipline and planning in the work we do. It will enable us to grow and make the commitments we need to make. I don't think Jonathan would object, *per se*, but I want to make sure we frame it in a way that speaks to him. I also want to make sure it is a direction that you two are comfortable with. Because you two are at the core of our future." Mia and Arnold were now visibly engaged and excited. Lunch ended and the two felt that they really had an ally in Romi and that this could be an opportunity for them to really become an integral part of the museum.

Romi solidified his core support by moving them beyond getting their general approval to accepting the direction he wants to head. He moved them from buy-in to a state where they were willing to help him put his ideas in place. He got them actively engaged and committed to his agenda. He built a shared sense of purpose. He incorporated their influence and perspective, vis-à-vis Jonathan Edwards, to make them an important part of his change effort. Romi seems to be successful in solidifying his core coalition. This is vital as he begins to introduce his agenda to the more senior people in the organization.

❧

It is too easy to assume that people who buy in will remain on the same page as you throughout the process. People maintain their self-interest, hidden agendas, and assumptions even after they've given you initial support and buy-in. If the underlying motivations of your colleagues go unchecked, you run the risk of having your coalition become a diffuse collection of interests that never gains the critical mass to get results.

When you are solidifying support, you cannot overcommunicate. W. Edwards Deming once wrote (in his book *Out of the Crisis* [MIT Press, 2000]) that getting the purpose clear was half the battle. Too often, people who try to make things happen in their organization assume that everyone "gets it" the first time around and that the purpose of the coalition doesn't have to be restated. That couldn't be further from the truth. In fact, most people need to hear something a few times before it finally sinks in. When you communicate the purpose of the coalition clearly, succinctly, and often, you will make it easier for your coalition members to take that message to their constituency.

Work Out Differences

No matter how successful you are in building a coalition and solidifying support, you have to keep in mind that your coalition isn't going to remain a homogenous group. You may establish some preliminary consensus around a particular agenda, but over time, inevitable differences will arise among coalition members. You need to continually reassess the consensus of coalition members to assure that you can sustain a semblance of homogeneity that can keep your group together. There are always going to be differences of opinion about the objectives of the coalition or the approach used to meet those ends. You need to recognize this diversity, leverage it, and manage the conflicts that will inevitably surface within the group. If you don't take the time to work out issues that have the potential to spiral out of control you may damage the long-term viability of your coalition.

A conservative, a leftist, and a libertarian can agree on extended highway funding, but can they agree on the role of government? They can create short-term, issue-specific coalitions, but can they form a coalition for long-term change? In developing a vocabulary to mobilize a coalition, your intent has to be clear.

You need to consider the extent to which coalition members support your common objectives. One way to gauge support is to evaluate the degree to which the coalition members share your strategic and tactical objectives. There may be varying support for different objectives (e.g., strategic and/or tactical objectives).

For example, you may find that some members don't necessarily disagree over the overall purpose of the coalition, but they have very distinct—and divergent—opinions about how the coalition should achieve its objective. You have to be sensitive to these differences in opinion because you will need to manage these internal conflicts in order to keep your coalition energized, functioning, and effective.

There are those who are Fully Supportive of your effort, including your vision of how to achieve it. These committed members share your strategic and tactical objectives and form the backbone of your coalition. There are others who joined your coalition, but once in, realize that they don't share your strategic or your tactical objectives. The danger of these Marginally Supportive members is that over time, they may become saboteurs and endanger your coalition from within. A third group consists of those who share your strategic objectives, but differ on tactics. These Strategically Supportive members may emerge as your coalition ideologues. Lastly, there are those who are comfortable with the coalition's current tactics, but are uncomfortable about the coalition's longer-term direction. These members are Tactically Supportive of your coalition. See the chart below for a map of your coalition membership:

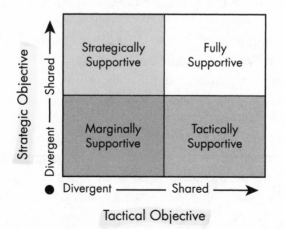

Recall the case of Bill Declan, the senior officer at a prestigious university trying to enter the online learning field (Chapter 5). Bill formed a coalition that was anything but homogenous.

First, there was Shara Puri, head of product development. Shara, an engineer by trade, was responsible for overseeing the technology staff and project managers who ensured that each course was delivered on time, on budget, and utilized the technology infrastructure that his group built and manages. Shara found all the meetings onerous and the discussions about the future of online learning, pedagogy, and academic quality to be more of a waste of time—mere arguing over semantics— when he could be working on delivering better technology and better development processes. Shara was a Tactically Supportive coalition member but felt Bill was too deferential to the faculty and learning officers.

Kurt Moyer, the learning officer, was responsible for developing the pedagogy and curricular requirements for all online courses. Kurt had a thankless job. He had to convince the university faculty that a standard pedagogy could be delivered across all online courses and that the model he'd chosen was a superior one to competing e-learning programs. Kurt was a key ally for Bill. Kurt was the primary liaison with the faculty and, with a Ph.D. himself, had the academic integrity that earned the respect of the faculty. Kurt was a Strategically Supportive coalition member, but he thought that Bill was too slick and really didn't value the pedagogy highly. Bill's indifference to many of the issues around pedagogy created tremendous tension with the faculty. Kurt, too often, found himself in the middle—assuring the faculty that their concerns would be addressed, while pushing the project ahead in accordance with Bill's aggressive schedule.

Victoria Flores, senior member of the Arts and Sciences faculty, supported the online learning initiative early on. She was excited about the technology's potential and felt that Bill understood how the expanded use of online learning would increase her professional exposure. Victoria put her Comparative Nineteenth-Century American Literature course online and that process was time-consuming and rife with misunderstandings and fell short of Victoria's expectations. It seemed that Victoria's vision for her course and the reality of what was being offered to students was quite different. Nevertheless, Victoria was excited about the future of online learning. Academically, she was already raising her profile, having been invited to speak at a number of conferences about her experience with e-learning. Because Victoria was a long-time friend of Bill she was a Fully Supportive coalition member, even though she had some real issues related to the academic quality of the online presentation of her course.

Donald Frey was the head of marketing for the e-learning initiative. Frey was a veteran of the direct marketing world, having spent the last nine years working on the creative team for the direct marketing subsidiary of a global advertising agency. Donald's specialty was pharmaceutical and health care marketing. He found those fields share similar characteristics with higher education. Donald was hired by Bill and had been his loyal deputy. In the seven months since he was hired, Frey realized that Bill's ideas shifted from a direct-marketing emphasis to one that focused on direct sales to groups and large organizations. As a result, the direct marketing work was seen more as collateral support for the sales force, rather than the core of the initiative's marketing and sales strategy. Donald was a Marginally Supportive coalition member.

Bill Declan built himself a diverse coalition of support. It is clear how each person may or may not be fully committed to him and/or to the initiative. As Bill continued to guide his initiative and his coalition through the political maze of the university, he would need to be cognizant of those who are Marginally Committed (e.g., Donald Frey) and others who may only be Strategically or Tactically Committed. If he is not politically aware, he may be vulnerable to sabotage or defection by coalition members.

&

As a coalition leader, you need to manage the conflicting views and opinions of your coalition members. You'll need to do this through healthy dialogue with your coalition members and through careful framing and reframing of the issues your coalition faces. If you are unable to manage the divergent views within your coalition, you run the risk that infighting will eat away at the efficacy of your coalition. You may also find that dissatisfied coalition members may be vulnerable to increasing pressure from counter-coalitions. The challenge to your political competence as a coalition leader is to get the highest level of commitment from your coalition members; you need to achieve some semblance of consensus with regard to your coalition's strategic and tactical objectives.

When Abraham Lincoln was nearing the end of his first term in office, his coalition began to unravel. The Civil War dragged on much longer than the public and the administration expected. As the campaign for the 1864 election developed, General George McClellan was able to build a strong counter-coalition. Within the Lincoln coalition, anti-war and anti-abolitionist factions surfaced. The president's coalition was in jeopardy of falling apart over their differences.

Lincoln used political competence to keep those differences within his party from splitting the Republicans. He further solidified his coalition by effectively redefining and restating the purpose of his coalition. His efforts paid off, as Lincoln won the election over McClellan.

Even the most respected leaders have differences within their ranks. You won't be immune from factions and interest groups emerging in your coalition. You shouldn't assume that your coalition is 100 percent behind you. The fact is that every coalition has internal differences. You need to recognize that and proactively manage those differences. As your coalition grows, you have to make sure that the internal differences do not undermine your coalition or open the door to the influence of counter-coalitions.

The best way to work out differences among coalition members is through negotiation. You need to act as an ad hoc arbitrator. Once you realize where there are differences, you should help both sides understand how they benefit from working together and how they can both achieve their own agendas while the coalition achieves its agenda. This is easier said than done. It takes a fair amount of time, a lot of patience, and a tremendous amount of tact and timing. It is your function to make sure that your coalition doesn't unravel with infighting. The payoff for you is huge—the difference between your agenda being achieved and being on the losing end of a politically charged issue.

Bear in mind that coalitions are not necessarily permanent forces. In order to sustain a coalition, you need to emphasize to the coalition members the importance of the agenda and defend the agenda against the opposition. You engage in team building and create a sense of the collective. By doing this, you reduce the possibility of defection. Another way of reducing attrition is to constantly reinforce to members that the long-run payoff of supporting your effort is better than the payoff they would get by abandoning your effort or joining a counter-coalition. Lincoln was able to paint McClellan as a traitor to the coalition and to the public—a surefire method of rallying Lincoln supporters.

Diffuse Your Ideas and Network

In order to get results, you've solidified your coalition, you've worked out differences among initial members, and now you have to make sure that your coalition's ideas are diffused throughout the organization and accepted as part of the status quo. What you must remember is that your coalition is part of an influence network within the organization. In order to move your ideas throughout the organization, you've got to get your ideas beyond your initial coalition and move them into the network that runs throughout the organization. You diffuse your ideas by making sure that key members of the organization's influence network will support your coalition's initiative.

During this process of diffusion, you are looking for what Malcolm Gladwell describes as the "tipping point" (as discussed in his book *The Tipping Point: How Little Things Can Make a Big Difference* [Back Bay Books, 2002]), the moment when your idea reaches a large number of employees—or at least the right employees—so that your ideas are no longer shared by only a select few, but are pervasive and viewed positively throughout the organization.

When diffusing your coalition's ideas, your primary concern is to increase the number of people in the influence network who are favorably exposed to your coalition's ideas. To do this, you want to make sure coalition members network to propagate your ideas throughout the organization. Your coalition members are going to be the ones who have to go out and talk to others in the organization. They have to be able to translate your message to inspire further action from their network of colleagues. They are the proselytizers. They are your evangelists.

Diffusion of ideas by networking is why solidifying your core coalition and working out differences is so important. Think about the children's game of telephone. You whisper a message to the person next to you, and they whisper the message to the next person, and so on. By the time your message gets back around to you, its original meaning is garbled and unintelligible. This is the dynamic for many failed change efforts. The leader of the coalition relies on others to share the message with others in the organization, who, in turn, share that message with even more people.

If you haven't done your political homework to solidify your coalition and work out differences among coalition members, it is almost a given that your message will be misstated and misunderstood, even among your coalition members. If that happens, an altered form of your idea, perhaps unrecognizable to you, will permeate the organization and cause confusion both within the coalition and throughout the organization as a whole. In this case, it may be that your true ideas will never come to the surface and be accepted by the organization and that your coalition will disband. Your coalition members are invaluable to you in getting out the message. But if they don't know the message to carry out, your idea may never see the light of day.

In order to diffuse your ideas throughout the organization and engage new coalition members, you need to communicate your agenda consistently. The best way to get your ideas accepted, and in turn, diffused throughout the organization, is to actively network outside your coalition. Don't wait for leaders of other interest groups, other coalitions, other departments, to contact you. Once you've established your coalition, you can only diffuse your ideas by networking with key actors outside your coalition. To get broad acceptance that will allow for the diffusion of your ideas, the coalition may need to get explicit support from the CEO or senior managers or from outside experts.

Most coalitions want to get a very senior person to endorse their idea. In today's high-risk organizational world, finding explicit senior support for any initiative is like drilling for oil. If you get it, you may win big, but there are very few productive wells and many more dry ones.

If your coalition is going to pursue this strategy for diffusing your ideas, you'll need ample time. You need time to work your way up to the senior levels by sharing the coalition's ideas with others who can get your coalition closer to your targeted supporters. This means a lot of meetings, a lot of canceled meetings, and very careful political positioning. Remember, you are seeking a referral from someone—perhaps someone who doesn't know you or your coalition members well—who can introduce you to someone else who might get you to your target. In this context, what becomes critical is to use members of your coalition as your proactive networkers.

Over the last two decades, management consultants have become tools for senior people to legitimize their agendas. The bigger the name of the firm, the better the consultant's book has sold, the better they are to endorse your coalition's idea. The opinion and support of an outside expert can carry tremendous weight in an organization. This has become a favorite and effective strategy for leaders of change efforts to get their ideas across.

You'll need to do your political homework if your coalition is going to get the endorsement from outside experts. You'll have to carefully consider which experts you want to bring on board. Experts need to have appropriate expertise; they need to be perceived as being independent; and they need to be able to respond to questions or deflect criticism in a manner that builds confidence in others. Not every expert, even those from top-notch firms, fills the bill. If you would like to bring in outside experts as a way of diffusing your coalition's ideas throughout the organization, you'll need to do your homework and carefully manage how you introduce the expert and his point of view to others in your organization.

Taking Stock

Incorporating new coalition members may sometimes be the subtlest form of networking. The obvious supporters are already members of your coalition. The challenge is to discover where there are other potential supporters throughout the organization. While getting the endorsement of upper-level officials and experts is important, teasing out the endorsement of others in the organization may be just as crucial to diffuse your coalition's ideas.

Sometimes you may be working off leads. You found out that someone heard through the grapevine that another manager seems to like your ideas. So, you set up a meeting and discuss your agenda more fully. If it sounds like a lot of work and a lot of proactive sensing, then you're right! For those who thought that ideas diffused the moment you had a coalition, think again. Diffusing your ideas beyond the base coalition will take time, effort, and active networking. Only when you are successful in diffusing your ideas beyond your initial coalition will your agenda will become part of the organization.

Putting your ideas in place is a matter of solidifying your coalition, working out the difference, and networking and diffusing. Remember, even if you have a buy-in, you want to make sure that your coalition has a clear sense of common purpose. You want to make sure that differences will not tear your coalition asunder. Finally, you want to use networking as a way of diffusing your coalition's ideas throughout the organization. You can only make things happen when people in your coalition network throughout the organization and diffuse the coalition's ideas when they feel a sense of solidarity and commonality.

Chapter 11

Lead the Coalition

You have the right people on board. You've gotten the buy-in. You've established a coalition. You're starting to make things happen in the organization.

Now is the time when you have to sustain the momentum of your coalition. You need to ensure that people are motivated and continue moving toward the coalition's goal. You have to provide active leadership.

Coalition leadership is the ability to motivate and coordinate group members to pursue the same goals. As a political leader of a coalition, you are the one who has to remain fixed and purposeful. However, while looking ahead, you must look over your shoulder to make sure your coalition remains intact. Politically competent leaders understand that while they may initiate a vision or a goal, they can only get results with the assistance of others. It is not enough to mobilize your coalition; you need to sustain it. To do this, you have to provide strategic and tactical leadership, you need to prepare your coalition for the emergence of counter-coalitions, and you need to keep your coalition from becoming insular.

What Leadership Really Means

There is a mythology of leadership; it is as if a leader is someone who is a charismatic source of inspiration, the perpetual initiator of creative ideas and new challenges. People tend to mystify leadership and view it as a characteristic only the select few possess. But leadership, specifically political leadership, occurs on every level of organizations.* In every sector of the organization, there are individuals who make things happen by creating coalitions. Every sector has people who know how to bring others along. These individuals often do not stand out as the mythological heroes that are often heralded in the current leadership literature. They are often strategic, tactical, and pragmatic people who understand what needs to be done and who they need in their corner.

Some psychologists argue that the ability to lead is an inherent trait, based on personality. While this may be true to a certain degree, leadership, in most organizational contexts, is a

---

* While there are many books that discuss leadership (e.g., Bernard M. Bass, *Transformational Leadership* [Lawrence Erlbaum Associates, 1998]), the most appropriate analysis to accompany this book for anyone concerned with political leadership is James MacGregor Burns's *Leadership* (Perennial, 1978).

deliberate choice. A leader is that individual who chooses to act and a political leader is a person who realizes that in order to make anything happen, he or she will have to sustain the support of others. For these individuals, leadership is not a characteristic of their personality, but a tool that they apply when necessary. For these individuals, how to lead and when to lead is a conscious decision.

As a political leader of a coalition, you can make something happen, you can take a chance, because you have the support of your coalition members. But it is a two-way street. In order to get support, you need to deal with the strategic and tactical concerns of your coalition members. In doing this, political leaders convert those who are only strategically, tactically, and marginally supportive of the coalition's objectives into fully supportive and active members.

Members of your coalition may have somewhat different goals: broad, ideological, strategic goals or practical, nuts-and-bolts, tactical goals. Sure, Jeff, the HRIS director at a fund management firm, sought to build a coalition around implementing a central payroll processing activity, but he might find that some people view the coalition's charter narrowly (e.g., we exist to implement a central payroll processing function) as something more ambitious (e.g., we seek to digitize the company's human resources processes).

To a large degree, this is an issue of what kind of leadership role you want to play, or more specifically what kind of presentation you want to use. How are you going to present yourself to members of your coalition? Will you use a presentation appealing to the strategic concerns of your membership or a presentation appealing to their tactical concerns? Political leaders understand that the style of leadership is contingent on what needs to be accomplished in a given situation. They understand that in different situations they may need to present different leadership scenarios. They don't have one leadership style; instead, they have a repertoire.

Strategic Leadership

A political leader who makes a strategic appeal addresses the overall vision and broadest goals of the coalition. In doing so, such a leader stresses the sense of affiliation and a communalism of the coalition and constantly reinforces a common vision. The strategic presentation uses the vocabulary of goals. When you talk to someone strategically, you talk about the overarching goals you want to achieve: the most efficient human resources information system; a fifth-grade reading level for all students; a 12 percent across-the-board reduction in costs.

The language of strategy places a disproportionate emphasis on the mission and vision to keep the group intact. The strategic presentation demands an emphasis on feelings and passion—a sense of enthusiasm. You convey your optimism and belief that the goals are important to achieve and can be achieved. You use a dramatic rhetoric, with metaphors, analogies, and symbols. A strategic presentation is primarily motivational.

❧

Bill Declan stood at the podium in the Hayes Auditorium on campus. The eighty or so employees of the e-learning unit and roughly forty invited guests—faculty, administrators, coalition members, and others—listened intently to what he had to say.

"You are all here because of your interest in reinventing higher education in the twenty-first century. And I thank you for your support and commitment to achieving our goals. When we began this journey just nineteen months ago, the nay-sayers were the dominant voice among the crowd. Some said we couldn't deliver a high-quality program. Others said that no one would buy it. Still others said the technology would be a disastrous problem. Thanks to your persistence, we've proved them all wrong!" A few cheers, whistles, and claps came from the crowd.

"But we're not done," Bill continued. "Oh, no, we are far from finished. For when we are finished, we will find that everyone in the world of higher education will point to us as the people who led a renaissance in our field. As the institution that provided the roadmap to quality. As the pioneers in bridging technology and the development of profound knowledge. You are those pioneers. You are the ambassadors to the future of education. You are taking the same bold steps that the founders of our great university took more than a century ago! I stand in awe of all of you. When others were critical, you were believers. When others said 'no,' you said 'yes.' When the time came to put your reputation on the line, you stepped up with confidence and commitment.

"So let me tell you this: You are achieving our shared vision. You are moving this great institution to the brink of an unprecedented transformation: the reinvention of higher education. And as I stand here today, I will continue to support your efforts to the best of my ability and to continue to hold our fine organization up as the model for education in the twenty-first century. And we will not stop until our entire university says 'yes!' Thank you very much for your commitment! And now Kurt is going to take you through the latest improvement in our learning model."

Bill walked offstage and headed straight to the car that was waiting for him outside the auditorium. Diane, his assistant, accompanied him with messages and reminders.

"They loved the speech, didn't they, Di?"

"Oh, I think they did."

"Whenever I give one of those, I really feel like we are so close to achieving our goals."

"Well, you've made a great deal of progress."

"And when I see that diverse group out there in the auditorium—everyone totally behind this thing—it makes me think that we really are the only ones who 'get it.' But that will change."

Bill engaged his coalition with stirring messages. He focused on the big ideas. He was thinking strategically, and he provided his coalition with confirmation of their *raison d'être*. He inspired them and motivated them through using drama. Bill Declan was practicing the art of strategic leadership.

The jury, though, is out as to whether he can keep his coalition continuously inspired with words alone.

⚮

Strategic leaders are constantly inventing new ways of keeping their constituents thinking about "a brighter tomorrow" or the unique opportunities that are possible today. It is often the case that the strategic leader is a more symbolic leader than a hands-on manager. On the other hand, there are many strategic leaders who take active roles in implementation efforts.

The problem with relying on a strategic presentation is that often you may be seen as inflexible and self-aggrandizing. You need to avoid having your coalition members seen as having allegiance only to you, rather than to the organization as a whole. Furthermore, you need to be aware that you do not give a sense that your coalition is a self-contained cult, but rather a critical part of the whole organization. Finally, you shouldn't confuse inspiration with resources. No matter how motivating the vision, the truth is that an army also runs on its stomach. In terms of our discussion, a political leader must be strategic, but also tactical.

Tactical Leadership

A political leader who makes a tactical appeal is concerned with the specific means by which goals are going to be achieved. "How are we going to get something done?" In doing so, a tactical leader will emphasize a vocabulary of tasks. What are the specific tasks that need to be done and how will they be coordinated? When you talk to someone tactically, you spend a disproportionate amount of time listening, reassuring, and analyzing. You spend the bulk of your time telling people how they can go about accomplishing something and convincing them that you're capable of mobilizing the resources they'll need.

In order to get results, a tactical coalition leader has to scavenge for resources, allocate them, and supervise their appropriate use. Think of the tactical leader as the COO of the coalition. He operates within, and is the product of, the bureaucratic structure of the organization. The tactical leader makes things happen in the organization by making others believe that the change seems practical. In making things happen, a tactical leader makes change appear less risky by operating through the prescribed organizational channels. A tactical coalition leader's chief activity is articulating to the whole organization the benefits that the wider organization can expect from the efforts of the coalition. The tactical leader constantly has in mind the importance of linking the coalition to the organization.

ॐ

Bill Declan was a master at commandeering resources. He had an ability to convince people that his initiatives were the most important the organization had. In many cases, he was proven right. But getting the kind of seed funding he was seeking was a monumental task at this sprawling, budget-strapped university. University officials were considering a number of different investments that they needed to make. There were proposals for several building renovation projects, in addition to the serious consideration given to a new hotel and corporate conference center. Bill's online initiative was not the only e-learning project being undertaken by the university. The leaders of the other projects were trying to make a strong case to the administration to be the primary development project, worthy of the lion's share of the funding.

Bill's weakness was getting his coalition to work together. He operated at his best in one-on-one situations and when speaking to large groups. But when it came time to manage small groups, he had a hard time finding the balance between controlling activities and empowering the group to work things through together. For example, last week, Bill had called a meeting with his coalition to discuss how they would approach Leo Burnett's request for a course on "Creative Writing for Business."

Bill kicked off the meeting explaining the situation and informed the group that "Burnett wants to offer the course next month."

"Bill, that time frame is much too tight," Shara Puri said. "If we had a course that was already developed, it might be doable. But without a course in hand today, there's no way we can turn that around within a month! I'm happy to commit to a December launch."

Victoria Flores, the faculty member, chimed in. "I don't know about that, Shara. I think I could put something together pretty quickly. I've worked with other companies on something similar, so I have the material. It's just a case of pulling it together. I say we try it and see what happens."

"You can't just 'try it,' Victoria," interjected Donald Frey. "We have to go out there with a specific date and get commitments. We probably can deliver on the creative within your time frame, Bill, but we won't have adequate time to pull a good response rate."

Bill responded, "Well, Don, we won't need much direct marketing support on this one. It's a single-company program."

Kurt Moyer interrupted. "With all due respect, Bill, Shara's right. We don't have the time to pull off a high-quality program. This is a topic we've never done before—to an audience that's pretty new to us. I'm concerned that we won't be able to provide the kind of learning experience that customers expect from us without a little testing and working through the content."

"Kurt, are you saying that you don't think I can put together a high-quality program on this?" Victoria asked, feeling that Kurt was questioning her ability to deliver.

"Victoria, I'm not saying that. I'm simply saying that we don't know whether this kind of content will work well with our learning model. I think it could. But you know how these things work. You don't know until you try it."

Shara interjected again. "Bill, can't you negotiate with the Leo Burnett people to push their program off an extra month? If you can, we can deliver something that'll really knock their socks off." Others nodded encouragingly.

"No way. The Duke people have already committed to that time frame and will take the business away from us if we don't match their timing. This is our challenge: We're either up to the task or we miss a potentially huge opportunity."

Bill was clearly aggravated with the direction the discussion was headed. "Listen, we have a unique opportunity here and I'm not going to let this pass without giving it a shot. Here's what I want. Don, I want collateral materials for this course developed and drafts on my desk in two weeks. Victoria, you need to deliver a course outline to Shara, with supporting detail by next Thursday. Shara, you need to clear the decks for the next month so that we can deliver this program. Your people are going to have to work round the clock on this one, but it will be worth it. Kurt, I'd like to talk to you offline after this meeting. Just make sure Shara and Victoria are on track. Any questions?"

The room fell silent. Everyone looked around, their eyes glazed over.

Bill continued, "Great. Why don't we meet next Friday, same time, and check in on our progress?"

Kurt followed Bill out the door and the two walked over to Bill's office. "Well, that went well," Bill commented.

"You think so? I think you teed a few people off in there."

"Listen, Kurt. No offense, but if someone doesn't just step in to lay down the law sometimes, you academics will spend weeks discussing things and come up with nothing. Sometimes we have to just lay things out for people and demand performance."

"I understand what you are saying, Bill," reacted Kurt, "but I'm not sure we have the time to deliver what Leo Burnett wants. And I think everyone in the room felt that and now feels a pressure to deliver something that is unreasonable to expect."

"Don't worry about it, Kurt. It'll work out just fine."

Bill shifted from his big vision of e-learning to a tactical leader of the initiative. The question was whether his tactical leadership approach would be as effective as his strategic leadership seems to be. By pointing out this corporate sales opportunity with Leo Burnett, Bill introduced some grim reality to the e-learning coalition. Reinventing higher education is nice, but it needs to be done in corporate time frames. Bill, who comes from a corporate sales background, has always been comfortable sacrificing a little quality for a product that is "good enough." That's clearly not the case with many members of his coalition. By forcing the issue with the Leo Burnett opportunity, Bill seemed to be controlling his coalition a bit more than everyone was comfortable with.

~

Tactical leadership can backfire when you are incapable of establishing long-term commitment from members of the coalition or from the wider organization. Because of the transactional nature of tactical leadership, you may have difficulty articulating the "higher purpose" of the coalition because your focus remains on process, on facilitating exchange, and on managing the initiative. There are times when coalition members need to be reminded or assured of the greater good that a change is bringing about. Over time, without the tactical leader's reinforcement of the "greater good," coalition members' commitment can waver.

As a tactical leader, you need to be careful to make it appear that you are not controlling coalition members. If coalition members get the sense that they are being controlled, they may abandon the coalition or turn into passive skeptics. Few individuals will join a coalition to help you out. They join as a means of achieving their own agendas—so you need to make sure that they have the freedom to support the effort in a way that they are comfortable with.

Successful Coalition Leadership

Successful coalition leadership, like leadership in any organization, combines strategy and tactics. The most effective coalition leaders are able to consistently and effectively communicate the purpose of the coalition, while doing the necessary "blocking and tackling." Leading a coalition isn't an either/or proposition. If you lack strategic leadership, your coalition may go stale or you may kill the momentum. If you lack tactical leadership, too many details can fall by the wayside and also derail your efforts.

If you are a politically competent coalition leader, you will need to employ both strategies. You know that at times you need to lead your coalition by saying, "I'll get the resources we need." And at other times you need to remind members to pull on their inner strength, "We can do it. Just hang in there a little longer."

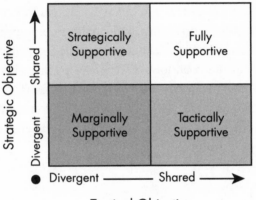

Tactical Objective

As a politically competent leader, you combine the strategic with the tactical and keep the coalition engaged and motivated with a compelling, well-articulated mission. When coalition members begin to stray, or move off track, you take them back to the core vision. If you lack strategic leadership, your coalition may forget its sense of purpose or mission. If you lack tactical leadership, you may fail to get the appropriate logistical support. If you lack both, your coalition will be rendered ineffective. If you have both strategic and tactical leadership, and know when to move seamlessly from one to the other, your coalition will have a politically competent leader.

The key to political leadership is the agility to move from the strategic to the tactical. A politically competent leader knows not to overplay one over the other. Franklin Delano Roosevelt is a classic example of the politically competent leader. (For an analysis of his leadership, see James MacGregor Burns's book *Roosevelt: The Lion and the Fox* [Harvest Books, Harcourt, Inc., 1984].) At times he led his New Deal coalition by appealing to the broader sense of mission. At other times, he engaged in the minutiae of cutting a deal. Roosevelt adapted his leadership presentation to the situation. When it came to establishing the New Deal, he was the broker, the tactical leader. When it came to dealing with the war, he was the preacher, the strategic leader.

The same is true in organizations. Working on the most micro-level of your department or at the highest levels of the organization, as a politically competent leader, you must ask yourself, given the situation, what type of language, what rhetoric, what presentation you need to choose.

In some instances, one leader isn't enough. You are aware of your strengths and weaknesses. If you are a strong strategic leader, you may find it necessary to bring a tactical leader on board to complement your strength. If you are a strong tactical leader, but find strategic presentation difficult, you may want to add a strategic leader to your coalition. Think of the visionary in your organization who doesn't work well with bureaucratic details or the bureaucrat who knows where every body is buried, but cannot articulate the vision. Think of the engineer who knows the technology cold, but cannot express its potential. Think of the marketing expert who understands the potential, but knows nothing about the technology needed to develop it.

⋘

Over the next month Bill Declan pushed his coalition hard.

Almost miraculously, the organization won the program from Leo Burnett and delivered the "Creative Writing for Business" course on time. The process pushed the coalition to its limits. They worked in the kind of time frame that was foreign to the university and made qualitative choices that would never have been made by the bricks-and-mortar institution.

The success had a ripple effect well beyond Bill's unit. They had built a real legitimacy within the university community and were now being talked about in positive ways across departments. There was still a healthy group of skeptics. But Bill's ability to inspire the troops and deliver on ambitious tactical goals built a tremendous store of political currency. An increasing number of faculty members were coming to Bill with proposals for online courses. And the salespeople now had a fairy tale success story to cinch more sales.

Bill provided the coalition with the strategic, visionary leadership that got the group excited. Then, he demonstrated the tactical leadership needed to deliver results. He had done the kind of internal fighting for resources and creating perceptions of success that enabled his coalition to be successful and gain momentum.

But Bill may have overlooked the cost of this success. In the course of delivering in intense time frames, the coalition members had slugged it out and beat each other up a bit. While they were regarded as quite successful, everyone was weary from internal battles. Like many successful ventures, the coalition members began believing in their success, perhaps more than they had a right to.

Counter-Coalitions

Effective coalition leadership isn't only about getting the strategy and tactics right. There are two important dynamics that political competence demands: You have to be aware of counter-coalitions and the insularity within your own coalition. Failure to be aware of counter-coalitions and of the tendency of coalitions to become insulated can derail the most effective leader. Failure to be aware of these two forces will guarantee that your coalition will be a short-term phenomenon, unable to get results over the long term.

It is inevitable that counter-coalitions will emerge. Leaders of counter-coalitions may believe that their agenda is superior to yours. You may think that over time others will come around to seeing things your way. You might hope that as your agenda becomes successful, that success will shield you from criticism. The reality is that there are always critics and multiple perspectives on any issue. It is not a question of "if," but of "when" a counter-coalition will emerge.

Politically competent leaders recognize the inevitability of counter-coalitions. They understand that by building their coalition, a counterforce will likely surface. In other words, the very success of your effort could, in fact, make you more vulnerable to challenging counterforces. Your responsibility is to recognize the existence of counter-coalitions. You need to understand the opposing perspectives, rather than brush them off as inconsequential, and leverage the strength of your coalition to pre-empt any efforts to derail your agenda.

Preparing for and responding to counter-coalitions is easier said than done. Counter-coalitions will emerge and their potential power is easy to underestimate. More often than not, you will dismiss their potency until it is too late. You need to have people out there, monitoring dissenting activity. You need to interpret activity of counter-coalitions, understand their arguments, and assess their strength—and their potential strength.

❧

Recall Donald Frey, the direct marketing manager hired by Bill Declan for his e-learning initiative. When Donald was hired, Bill was moving the e-learning activities toward a direct marketing model. Over time, Bill's agenda shifted toward one emphasizing corporate sales. Donald lost his positional power and resented Bill, as he felt betrayed. Donald had been closely enough involved in the Leo Burnett program to know that it was by no means the smooth and model program that Bill touted.

Over the next few months, Donald Frey talked with others at the university. He cultivated faculty who continued to oppose Bill's agenda. He got the attention of key members of technical support who were burnt out by Bill's push for the Leo Burnett project. Slowly, Donald formed the nucleus of a counter-coalition, one that questioned the corporate sales model and tried to make the case that the university shouldn't be "selling out" but instead be committed to bringing cost-effective, high-quality education to those who might never be able to come onto campus.

Donald's agenda was compelling. Vivian Lo Porto approached Bill one day and mentioned Donald's maneuvering. Bill responded, "Viv, I brought Donald Frey into this organization. He may be a bit upset because we're not going after those onesies and twosies. But he's got no power at the university. Sure, people may give him their ear. But his bickering isn't going anywhere."

Bill made a classic mistake. He underestimated the presence and potential impact of a counter-coalition.

Keeping Your Coalition from Becoming Insular

Every organization, regardless of size, faces this problem at some point: They become successful and their success gets the better of them. It is easy to get complacent. Once you've solidified your coalition, you have to guard against psychological inertia, a sense of complacency that comes with success, a sense that you've won on this particular issue and therefore are quite invulnerable. Poor coalition leaders develop an illusion of invincibility. They get the sense that they can triumph in spite of danger signs. There is a certain drunkenness of power that comes with success—a sense that you can overcome anything. This sense of invulnerability allows leaders to ignore warnings and to rationalize mistakes. It leads to the development of self-righteousness, and an inability to reflect or be self-critical.* Others may raise warnings that will be ignored. This is the danger of an insular coalition.

In this instance, the coalition leaders and members shift from viewing the coalition as a means to achieving a particular end to viewing the coalition as an end in itself. There is a sense that the very coalition that was meant to create momentum becomes a self-serving oligarchy, where leadership is primarily concerned with retaining their own power and pushing their own specific agenda. At this point, coalition leadership and the coalition itself become susceptible to the forces of counter-coalitions because at this point, they

---

* The ideas in this section are greatly adopted from Irving Janis's work, as developed in his book *Groupthink: Psychological Studies of Policy Decisions and Fiascoes* (Houghton Mifflin, 1982), which examines groupthink in policy arenas. For example, his policy analysis of such issues as Vietnam, the Bay of Pigs, and other critical decisions is based on his assumption that groupthink creates a certain insularity among entities like coalitions.

can easily be accused of having a narrow focused vision and having lost their sense of drive and momentum.*

At Bill Declan's monthly meeting of senior coalition members, he kicked off the meeting with a note. "This is a note I received today from one of the faculty. Let me read it to you. 'Dear Bill, I'm really impressed with the online work you are doing and would like to hear more about it. I was skeptical for a time, but now am beginning to see the possibilities.' We're starting to get a lot of these." A colleague agreed, "Yes, we are really getting raves from all over the university. You can really feel the momentum building." A third voice interjected, "I've heard a lot of good things, too. But I've also heard that there's a groundswell of criticism and a small movement to try a different approach within the university."

"Oh, that's such B.S.," Bill responded. "We've built up so much currency with the administration that they'd be crazy to consider another model. And, anyway, there's not a better model out there, right, people!?" The group roared.

---

* The notion that leaders will try to sustain power and dominate through oligarchies was first developed in Robert Michels's classic 1915 work *Political Parties*, a study of the oligarchic tendencies of modern democracy. Michels reminds us of how insular coalitions may often become. This notion is examined in an organizational context by Seymour Lipset et al. (*Union Democracy*, Anchor, 1956) in the study of oligarchic coalition control in contemporary unions. This Michels-Lipset tradition, combined with Irving Janis's work on groupthink, cautions leaders to be guarded against inertia and insularity.

"Listen, I wouldn't worry about those critics. They've always been there and they always will. But now, they're just jealous. And they really don't have a leg to stand on." Bill concluded and moved on to some of the tactical issues relating to the Leo Burnett project.

ॐ

Notice how all the data being gathered is internal? Notice how any suggestion of dissent is struck down as irrelevant and even untrue? These are telltale signs that a coalition is becoming insular and complacent.

As a politically competent leader, you will need to encourage open dialogue and will constantly try to incorporate information from the outside. You may even go so far as to make sure that your group listens to outsiders who may not agree with your coalition's agenda or those who may be aware of the positions of others in the organization. You will need to constantly play the role of devil's advocate, pointing out flaws in your coalition's position, in order to get others in your coalition to continually question their approach. Such tactics obviously have to be done carefully because if they are overdone, you can undermine the very coalition you created.

Leading and sustaining a coalition is hard work—and it is the difference between making things happen in your organization and getting little or nothing done. You may have worked hard and built yourself a nice coalition of support. But you now need to do something with that support. You know you need to provide the currency of political competence: strategic and tactical leadership. Just as important for leading a coalition is your ability to anticipate and respond to counter-coalitions and, also, to lead your coalition in a way that prevents it from becoming too insular. Your ability to put all these pieces together will determine whether you're a hero or a casualty—whether you will survive to implement your next agenda.

Conclusion

The Politically Competent Leader

When push comes to shove, leadership comes down to a simple issue: Are you able to take ideas and translate them into action? As was said in the beginning, good ideas are abundant. The problem is putting ideas in place. In the final analysis, as a leader you will be judged on whether you could put good ideas into action. After reading this volume, you know that putting good ideas in place involves political processes and political skills—to a large degree, leadership is an issue of your political competence. First, it involves your ability to map the terrain—anticipate the reaction of others, identify allies and resistors, analyze their goals, and understand their agendas. Second, once you identify allies and resistors, you get them on your side by establishing your credibility, justifying your action, and getting their support. Finally, you've got to make things happen—you get the buy-in, put your ideas in place, and lead the coalition.

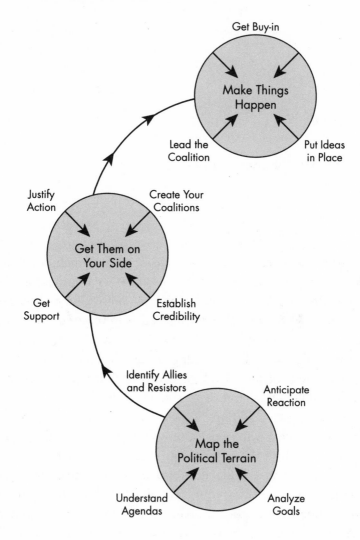

Mastering only certain parts of the process outlined here will lead to, at best, only partial success, and is more likely to result in failure. The following sections describe several types of figures who fall down in one stage or another of the process of generating and implementing change.

The Political Analyst

When you've only mapped your political terrain, but failed to build a coalition, you are a Political Analyst. Political Analysts are those who are able to anticipate the reactions of others and understand their agendas, but they have an inability to get others on their side. They are not capable of going through the dialogue and interaction that is necessary to build a coalition. That doesn't mean Political Analysts don't try to make things happen in organizations. They do try, but they think that by simply identifying the interests of individuals and key units, they've done enough. They don't realize that mapping is only the first step to making things happen.

అ

Recall the case of George Irwin at the Broome County Sisterhood Hospital (Chapter 4). George did a terrific and thorough job of identifying his allies and resistors and analyzing their change agendas. He was well on his way to politically competent leadership. But then something happened. George heard through the rumor mill that a few people were dismissing his idea for satellite networks as unrealistic. In fact, two of those people were Monroe Moore and Jane Cook. Monroe was the only other person, besides himself, that George identified as having a Revolutionary agenda. And Jane chose a Developer agenda, but she was someone who George felt he could bring on board.

This information spooked George and he lost confidence that he could get his idea adopted. As a result, George never tried to get a meeting with Monroe or Jane, as he didn't want to be rejected. Instead, George met with a few marginal players and he spent more time talking to his resistors than to his potential allies.

George has very low self-esteem. He spends all his time talking to skeptics because he is trying to turn them around and he knows they are clearly opposition. They were all too willing to reinforce why his satellite clinics were a bad idea. George argued passionately with them, but he wasn't able to make a strong enough case to bring them on board. More likely than not, they looked around and didn't see anyone supporting George's effort. George didn't call on Monroe or Jane because of lack of confidence.

George pushed ahead without a coalition. He developed a business plan and got on the agenda at a scheduled management meeting. George presented his idea and plan at the meeting and it got ugly. It turned out that many people at the meeting hadn't heard about the plan from George and they were surprised that he didn't take the time to talk to them privately beforehand. He presented his plan and it was met with an hour and a half of questions. By the end of the meeting, George had lost the few people who might have initially supported his effort. By going public before having a group of supporters on his side, George had left himself out there alone and his satellite clinic initiative—despite being an excellent idea—was quickly being taken off the table.

The Consensus Builder

You see Consensus Builders everywhere in your organization. These are folks who do their political mapping, understand the terrain of allies and resistors, and who spend the remainder of their time building coalitions of support. The problem is, that's where they stop. Consensus Builders never seem to be able to get past that stage. They are unable to mobilize their supporters in a way that actually makes things happen.

Consensus Builders have very strong process capabilities. They have the ability to prolong meetings into marathon sessions with their diatribes and their need to "talk ideas to death." Consensus Builders are often among the most beloved and integral players in the organization. Often, they can tip the scale in their favor due to their ability to get people on board an initiative. In addition, their generally favorable reputation in the organization can often attract the resources and people that a coalition needs to get results.

But Consensus Builders are taken with this stage of the political process. They bask in the thought of a meeting. They'll end every encounter with, "We should have a meeting to discuss this." Consensus Builders have the best of intentions to get results. They are just unable to get to the next level. But if there are too many Consensus Builders—and you've seen this before—the organization will spend an inordinate amount of time meeting, discussing, evaluating, and never really accomplishing much of anything.

∽

Let's return to Jerome Claywar and his effort to implement a small school initiative into the metropolitan city school system (Chapter 8). Jerome had done a thorough job of doing his political homework. He understood, as well as anyone could, the complex dynamics of effecting change in a city school system. He identified the key people and groups who would likely support his agenda and he identified those who would likely resist it.

Through a series of meetings over the next several months, Jerome met with all of his potential allies and many of his skeptics. He was extremely effective in getting them on board to support his effort. Jerome's credibility, the way he gets along well with people, and the conviction of his idea all went a long way to persuading others that this was a viable and needed initiative.

Over the next two months, Jerome cycled back to these groups. He gave them an update on who was now on board and just kept the conversation going. Jerome even brought on a few new and influential community leaders. He was feeling very upbeat as he knocked on the door of Jerry Mayfield, the school superintendent. This was his third meeting with Jerry and while he had been very receptive to Jerome the last two times, this time he was visibly bothered. After Jerome and Jerry spoke for fifteen minutes, Jerry finally spoke up. "Jerome, what the heck is going on here? For the past four months you've been coming into my office and telling me about all these people who are on board with your small school effort. But I don't see anything happening! How is this thing actually moving forward? I'm inclined to be supportive, Jerome, but I don't know what it is that I'm supporting."

Jerome bristled. "Jerry, these things take time. I don't have to tell you that there are a lot of dicey political issues and I want to make sure that we've ironed them out before taking the next step."

"I understand, Jerome, better than anyone. But you've got to start getting people mobilized if you want this thing off the ground."

For the next two months, Jerome got a few of his supporters to begin to pursue different aspects of the small school initiative. He sent them out to take care of some first steps that needed to be accomplished. After a few weeks, Jerome got a call from the mayor's office. "Jerome, we've had four people coming here—telling us that you sent them—all asking for the same information and asking for a meeting with the city council. What is going on here? I have to tell you that the mayor is getting concerned. You've gotten a lot of people excited about the small school effort, but nothing is happening. People are starting to ask the mayor about progress and he hasn't heard a thing from you or anyone else. Is this thing moving forward, Jerome?"

Jerome's small school initiative wasn't moving forward. Jerome had gotten all the pieces in place, but now needed to mobilize and lead his supporters. But he was spinning his wheels. He lacked a plan and the political competence to lead a coalition through effective implementation. Jerome Claywar was a master Consensus Builder. The small school initiative lay dormant because Jerome was unable to provide the strategic and tactical leadership needed to implement his idea.

The Politically Competent Leader

Politically Competent Leaders are the ones who put all three components of the political process in place: They map the terrain, they get people on their side, and they get results. They do their up-front homework to map the political terrain, understand who is likely to be on their side and who is likely to resist them. They get people on board and build a coalition. Then, they lead the coalition to get results.

Politically Competent Leaders typically fall within two categories—those who build very narrow coalitions and those who build broad coalitions of support. Those who build very narrow coalitions face the danger that their leadership—and their change effort—may stand on shaky ground. Often, these Politically Competent Leaders pursue and effect change that the broader organization doesn't necessarily want or support. Nevertheless, their political competence enables them to push their agenda through. Think of leaders like Al Dunlap (during his tenure at Sunbeam) and Jack Welch (in his early years at GE).* Both pursued highly unpopular agendas, had very narrow but powerful coalitions, and led their coalition effectively to realize their change agenda. Dunlap was unable to broaden support for his change efforts, while Welch was able to do so—which put Welch into the second category of Politically Competent Leader: those who are able to get many people on their side and build a broad coalition of support.

Politically Competent Leaders who build broad coalitions of support not only push their agenda through, but also have a solid base from which they can lead and pursue future agendas. Sometimes, as in the case with Jack Welch, broad support develops over time. Other times, a Politically Competent

---

* For a discussion of Dunlap, see John Byrne's book *Chainsaw: The Notorious Career of Al Dunlap in the Era of Profit-at-Any-Price* (HarperBusiness, 1999). For Jack Welch's side of his story, see his book (cowritten with John Byrne) *Jack: Straight from the Gut* (Warner Books, 2001).

Leader will develop a broad coalition early on and, over time, solidify and expand on that. Of the two categories of Politically Competent Leaders, those who build a broad coalition as opposed to a narrow one will have more idiosyncrasy points when things don't go right.

↝

Romi Cruz, the director of the Deacon County Museum of Contemporary Art (Chapter 10), was able to secure the support of Mia Stephens and Arnold Hynes, the two curators who worked for Jonathan Edwards. Romi was also able to get Roberta Jones, the director of membership, to support his change effort.

With those three on board, Romi began to mobilize them. He was able to get the curators to negotiate with Jonathan to reallocate funds among their collection and to sell certain nonstrategic assets. Roberta agreed to cut spending on certain membership drives in return for an additional budget for highly targeted partnership efforts. Romi also got Roberta to use her influence and friendships with the people in the education department to scale back their expenditures.

Over four months, Romi reduced the operating budget by 7 percent and started to restructure the museum's support functions. Romi's early moves paid off. Membership increased and the museum received some good press for their new sculpture exhibit. And an educational program aimed at senior citizens became one of Deacon County's most popular community events.

Romi used these successes to make more fundamental changes in the way the museum was organized. He was able to push through some additional budget cuts, while increasing investment in targeted curatorial areas. By the end of the year, Romi pushed his agenda, achieved early successes, and he was well on his way to taking a firm hold on the leadership of the museum.

Reducing Risk Through Political Competence

Robert Rubin, United States Treasury Secretary from 1995 to 1999, recently stated that a major insight he gained while an undergraduate at Harvard, one that stayed with him throughout his career, was that everything was uncertain; at best, he could only make probabilistic decisions.

As he puts it in his book *In an Uncertain World* (Random House, 2003): "Once you've internalized the concept that you can't prove anything in absolute terms, life becomes all the more about odds, choices, and trade-offs." Knowing that he couldn't know everything, he knew that he had to estimate the consequences of his actions. This is consistent with the thinking of the Nobel Prize–winning economist, Herbert Simon, which emphasizes that because we can't know everything, any decision we make is bounded by the information we have, and therefore, there is no such thing as a perfect decision.*

In organizations, you know you need to make a decision. You know that you need to initiate action. You try to make a satisfactory decision given the limitations of your capital, time restraints, and other resources. But someplace, deep inside of you, you're not sure about the consequences. You hope you made the best decision, but you know you could have easily made other decisions. No matter what course of action you take, there is risk. This is the reality leaders face every day when they try to make things happen in organizations.

---

* Herbert Simon makes a distinction between satisfying and optimizing. In his terms, "In terms of satisfying and optimizing . . . are labels for two broad approaches to rational behavior in situations where complexity and uncertainty make global rationality impossible. In these situations, optimization becomes approximate optimization—the description of the real-world situation is radically simplified until reduced to a degree of complication that the decision maker can handle. Satisfying approaches seek this simplification in a somewhat different direction, retaining more of the detail of the real-world situation, but settling for a satisfactory, rather than an approximate-best, decision." (Herbert A. Simon, *Models of Bounded Rationality: Behavioral Economics and Business Organization, Vol. 2,* The MIT Press, 1982, pg. 417.)

If you keep trying to optimize, rather than making a *satisfying* solution, you may find that you will search forever. Your aspiration for the optimal solution may lead you to seek out one alternative after another. When you *satisfy*, you maintain that your decision is not optimal and, in fact, that there may be no optimal solution. Therefore, you consciously restrict aspirations and your search for alternatives.

Every action anyone takes carries the risk of failure. The goal of the politically competent leader is to reduce the risk of failure and increase the chance that his initiative is successful. Leaders face two predominant risks: their decision to take action may be based on inadequate information and the decision itself may increase their political vulnerability by opening them up to criticism.

You're at risk if you do not have a process in place that allows you to gather as much information as you can in order to make the best decision you can, given the constraints. Because there are no best decisions in organizations, you are open to criticism—and politically vulnerable—whenever you make a decision.

Politically competent leaders reduce the risk of acting on inadequate or incomplete information by getting as many people as possible on their side. The process of identifying allies and resistors and then moving on to negotiate with them by discussing one issue versus multiple issues, establishing credibility, justifying action—assures that political leaders will create a dialogue that will force much valuable information to the surface. The politically competent leader is able to make a decision—a better decision, if not a perfect one—and take action based on much more information than a leader who just forges ahead with his idea without getting people on his side. The coalition-building process, in and of itself, reduces the risk of making a decision based on spotty or one-sided information. Building a coalition is a search process for the best solution.

The act of building a coalition, getting people together, solidifying and expanding the coalition, makes the politically competent leader less vulnerable to criticism. When critics attack, the coalition makes it easier for the politically competent leader to deflect criticism and move ahead with his plan. It is easier to attack a single person standing alone than a leader who has built up a broad base of support throughout the organization.

Politically Competent Leaders are often rewarded for their efforts. They are praised throughout their organization and they build a tremendous amount of political currency, allowing them to take on future projects with greater risk. Politically Competent Leaders are protected from criticism and recrimination, while the Political Analyst and the Consensus Builder are not so well positioned. This is not to say that Politically Competent Leaders can rest on their laurels. Far from it. Politically Competent Leaders need to leverage the halo effect to expand their coalition of support and to prepare for the next project.

Index

Relevant Readings

Allison, Graham and Philip Zelikow. *Essence of Decision: Explaining the Cuban Missile Crisis* (2nd Edition). New York: Longman/Addison Wesley, 1999.

Axelrod, Robert. *The Evolution of Cooperation*. New York: Basic Books, 1985.

Bacharach, S. and E. J. Lawler. *Organizational Politics*. Stamford, Conn: JAI Press, 2000.

Bossidy, Larry and Ram Charan. *Execution: The Discipline of Getting Things Done*. New York: Crown Business, 2002.

Burns, James MacGregor. *Roosevelt: The Soldier of Freedom 1940-1945*. New York: Harvest/HBJ Book, 2002.

Caplow, Theodore. *Two Against One: Coalitions in Triads*. New York: Prentice-Hall, 1968.

Caro, Robert A. *Master of the Senate: The Years of Lyndon Johnson*. New York: Knopf, 2002.

Gamson, William A. *Power and Discontent*. Homewood, Ill.: Richard d Irwin, 1968.

Gardner, Howard. *Changing Minds: The Art and Science of Changing Our Own and Other People's Minds*. Boston: Harvard Business School Press, 2004.

Hirschman, Albert O. *The Rhetoric of Reaction: Perversity, Futility, Jeopardy*. Cambridge, Mass.: Belknap Press of Harvard University Press, 1991.

Kanter, Rosabeth Moss. *The Change Masters*. New York: Touchstone/Simon & Schuster, 1983.

Katzenbach, Jon R., ed. *The Work of Teams*. Boston: Harvard Business School Press, 1998.

Kotter, John P. *Leading Change*. Boston: Harvard Business School Press, 1996.

March, James G. and Herbert A. Simon. *Organizations*. New York: John Wiley & Sons, Inc., 1958.

McCullough, David. *John Adams*. New York: Touchstone / Simon & Schuster, 2002.

Pfeffer, Jeffrey. *Managing with Power: Politics and Influence in Organizations*. Boston: Harvard Business School Press, 1994.

Raiffa, Howard. *The Art and Science of Negotiation*. Cambridge, Mass.: Belknap Press of Harvard University Press, 1982.

Rogers, Everett M. *Diffusion of Innovations* (5th Edition). New York: Free Press, 2003.

Senge, Peter M. *The Fifth Discipline: The Art and Practice of the Learning Organization*. New York: Currency Doubleday, 1994.

Tedlow, Richard S. *Giants of Enterprise: Seven Business Innovators and the Empires they Built*. New York: HarperBusiness, 2001.

Vecchio, Robert P., ed. *Leadership: Understanding the Dynamics of Power and Influence in Organizations*. Notre Dame: University of Notre Dame Press, 1997.

About the Author

SAMUEL B. BACHARACH is the McKelvey-Grant Professor in the Department of Organizational Behavior at the School of Industrial and Labor Relations at Cornell University. He is the director of Cornell's New York City–based Institute for Workplace Studies and the Smithers Institute. He is the author and editor of over twenty books on management, organizational behavior, and industrial relations. His research has been published in most of the major academic journals.

Get Them on Your Side is Professor Bacharach's effort to transform his thirty years of academic research on negotiation, organizational behavior, industrial relations, and leadership into a book that is practical and accessible to practitioners. His primary concern is to demonstrate to individuals that they are capable of political competence and coalition building and that these skills are teachable. He believes that change can only be brought about by proactive leaders who have developed the skills of political competence.

Professor Bacharach teaches the discipline of political competence to executives, politicians, managers, and students around the world. Besides teaching these concepts in-depth to undergraduate and graduate students at Cornell's School of Industrial and Labor Relations, he develops and runs workshops and engages in individual consulting and coaching. Recently, his research has been adapted into four online courses on proactive leadership and offered to the public as a certificate program by eCornell. Seminars and workshops based on this material are offered through Cornell ILR's Management Programs.

He lives in downtown Manhattan with his wife and son, where he also spends time dabbling in art criticism and novel writing.

To learn more about Professor Bacharach, the concepts in this book, and the online courses offered through eCornell and workshops and seminars provided by Cornell ILR's Management Programs, visit his Web site at *www.getthemonyourside.com*.